Making Deals with God

A Verse By Verse Ministry International Publication

Stephen Armstrong

Copyright © 2021 by **Stephen Armstrong**

All rights reserved. No part of this publication may be reproduced, distributed, or transmitted in any form or by any means, without prior written permission.

Unless otherwise noted, all Scripture quotations are taken from the New American Standard Bible ® (NASB), copyright © 1960, 1962, 1963, 1968, 1971, 1972, 1973, 1975, 1977, 1995 by The Lockman Foundation. Used by permission. www.Lockman.org.

Making Deals with God / Stephen Armstrong
ISBN-13: 9798505975251

This book is dedicated to people around the world who hunger for the Truth found in God's written word.

This book is also dedicated to Pastor Stephen Armstrong who founded Verse By Verse Ministry International and lived his life with eyes for eternity.

May God be pleased with what is taught in these pages and guide the readers in their pursuit of God's Truth.

CONTENTS

Foreword 2
Making Deals with God 7
Quid Pro Quo Prayer? 37
Give and Get Prosperity 55
Limitless Healing 73
Human-Centered Evangelism 89
God vs. Satan 119
Experience Over Scripture 135
Works Cited 153
About the Author 157

Foreword

Everyone appreciates self-help books. In a chaotic world filled with upheaval, disappointment, and struggles, the opportunity for our best life now is irresistible. The successful self-help book formula starts with an attractive expert pitching an enticing blend of pop psychology, new age mysticism, alternative medicine, and pseudo-religion and promising us the self-actualized life of our dreams. If we read the book and follow the advice, good things will follow (or so they claim).[1]

Self-help advice has always sold well, but recently a new type of self-help book has become especially popular: *Christian* self-help books. Christian self-help books usually aren't classified in the self-help genre, but they're built upon the same, reliable formula pioneered by their secular variety. Christian self-help books have updated traditional self-help advice for a religious-minded audience by incorporating biblical references that lend credibility and authority to their claims.

These books have become tremendously popular among the faithful, and they transform obscure pastors and motivational speakers into world-renowned life-coaches and purveyors of optimism and blessing — but the effect of these books is very different from their promises.

The Christian self-help genre is a rogue's gallery of charlatans and frauds who make unbiblical promises and prey on ignorant and desperate Christians. Among the many false claims made in these books are assertions that God always rescues believers from difficulties in life, heals us repeatedly from every disease, and grants us financial windfalls whenever we ask.[2] With promises like that, it's no wonder these books are popular! Who wouldn't like a god who grants such wishes? We would do well to remember that when something sounds too good to be true, generally, it is.

Christian self-help books peddle an unbiblical view of our relationship with God based on a false theology that maintains God responds to our desires and can be made to do our will. Generations of Disney movies told us when we rub the genie's lamp or wish upon a star, our dreams come true, and Christian self-help peddles a similar story. It portrays God as a genie who waits patiently for His followers to "release" His favor, and if we apply the right methods, we can unlock or release His favor with a bonanza of blessings. Moreover, when we think and act according to the instructions, the books say, God will be obligated to respond in kind.

Unsurprisingly, this news is too good to be true. Christian-styled self-help is really an elaborate con game where faithful sheep are fleeced by false shepherds. The con is easy to spot, because self-help theology promises the impossible. Simply put, humanity *can't* manipulate God, much less force Him to do our bidding. The Lord God is the beginning and the end of all things, the source of all knowledge and power in the universe, the Author of all history and the Judge of all creation. As the Creator, God is far above His creation (of which humanity is a part), and therefore, any teaching suggesting the Creator serves His creation is profoundly flawed and self-evidently wrong.

Breaking someone free from the spell of this false teaching begins by asking one fundamental question: *who's in charge?* While Christian self-help would respond by saying *we* can control our spiritual dividends from God, the Bible consistently responds with a different answer: *God alone is sovereign.*

The term *sovereignty* refers to God's supreme and undisputed power. The Bible teaches that God is sovereign over everything in His Creation, meaning there is no other source of power or authority or truth. God alone determines all outcomes in all circumstances throughout all history, and God's immutable sovereignty is the Bible's rebuttal to the lies of Christian self-help.

Given the rising popularity of Christian self-help teaching (in various forms), it's time Christians had a strong, biblical rebuttal for all who might teach such heresy and for any who might fall victim to it. This book is an attempt to offer such a rebuttal by exploring what the Bible says about God's sovereignty in six areas of a Christian's faith and life:

- ***Quid Pro Quo Prayer?*** – Do our prayers direct or control God's decisions and actions?

- *Give and Get Prosperity?* – Does God promise to grant all believers monetary wealth in their life on earth?

- *Limitless Healing?* – Can our physical and psychological infirmities be remedied by a greater faith in God's willingness to grant healing?

- *Human-Centered Evangelism?* – Is our evangelistic success dependent upon our methodology and presentation style?

- *God vs. Satan?* – Do we attribute world tragedies and disasters to Satan, or does God rule over these, too?

- *Experience or Scripture?* – How does our faith in the sufficiency of God's Word guide our walk with Jesus?

In each area, we will consider what the Bible says about God's control and contrast that with what the world says about humanity's relationship with God. In the process, we'll expose the lies of transactional theology, the term we'll use for the Christian self-help heresy. In the end, it all comes down to understanding how God's creation relates to a sovereign God.

So, who's in charge? Let's find out.

CHAPTER ONE

Making Deals with God

The biblical view of God's sovereignty is under assault from a dangerous heresy that reduces the God of the universe to a benevolent genie who has the power to grant wishes. This new theology teaches that God's chief purpose in His relationship with His children is to grant us what we desire, and therefore He responds to our desires affirmatively — if we approach Him correctly. This teaching claims Christians have the power to turn on this tap of our blessing by thinking and acting a certain way toward God, like how a genie responds when a person rubs the lamp correctly.

Christians who come under the influence of this teaching often develop a self-centered view of their relationship with Christ. For this group, Jesus becomes a heavenly ATM dispensing endless riches and making dreams of financial independence possible. For the sick, Jesus is a 24-hour pharmacy offering miracle cures for every ailment. In times of tragedy, Jesus is a heavenly insurance policy protecting against disasters and indemnifying every loss.

A Christian will be assured these "blessings" as rewards for following Jesus, so long as he or she meets God's expectations for faith and tithing.

I call this heretical teaching *transactional theology*, because the teaching reduces a believer's relationship with God to a *quid pro quo* arrangement. A *quid pro quo* is Latin for "something for something," referring to an exchange of value between two parties in which each party's involvement is contingent upon the other's performance. Think of it as a "you scratch my back, I'll scratch yours" arrangement, and that's exactly how transactional theology imagines our relationship with God.

We give God what He wants, transactional theology teaches, and He will give us what we want. Specifically, we must show God our "faith" in Him to receive what we desire, and when we show enough faith, He will grant us anything we desire. In that sense, believers are said to have control over God, at least to the degree we can prompt Him to act on our desires. So, if you can imagine it and believe strongly enough that God will grant it to you, then it can be yours. In the parlance of transactional theology, if you "believe on God for *X"* (e.g., a car, a job, a spouse, etc.), God will grant your desire because your faith obligates Him to act. It's a *quid pro quo* arrangement: we do our part, and God will do His part.

It's not hard to see how Christian self-help teaching like this encourages carnality among believers by substituting the pursuit of fleshly desires for a life dedicated to holiness, self-sacrificial service, and sharing the true gospel of salvation by grace through faith in Jesus Christ. In place of these Christian goals, believers are told God approves of their lustful desires, but to quote the prophet Isaiah, "Woe to those who call evil good, and good evil" (Isaiah 5:20).

If this sounds like the plot from a Disney cartoon, you're not far from the truth. Transactional theology is little more than fairy tale masquerading as spiritual insight. As ridiculous as this teaching is, however, it entices and misleads many. In just a couple of generations, transactional theology has become an influential heresy in many churches around the world. Millions of believers have moved away from biblical truth to embrace a lustful, self-indulgent style of religion that diminishes God's power and purpose. What's worse, many *unbelievers* have joined these deceived churches without receiving the grace of God through faith in Jesus, because they bought into the transactional view that God helps those who help themselves.

To understand how transactional theology works, we need to appreciate its two key teachings or tenets that work together to peddle a false view of God and of the Christian faith in general.

Tenet #1: God Will Grant Us Our Desires

First, transactional theology asserts that God is inclined to grant us our personal desires in proportion to our expectation that He will do so. The more we believe God will give us what we desire, the more power or leverage we possess to compel God into granting those desires.

Should someone ask why God would obey our desires in this way, the false teachers will claim God's *faithfulness* requires that He grant us wealth, healing, etc., when we demonstrate faith in His potential to do so. Because we have shown "faith" in Him, He is obligated to reward our faith. In other words, He will be faithful because we are faithful to believe He is faithful — which is circular reasoning and the definition of a *quid pro quo* relationship. Notably, this is also the *opposite* of grace, because we are said to be deserving of favor from God.

Based on this *quid pro quo* logic, false teachers urge their audiences to dream big. Ask for the moon, they say, because God *must* grant our requests when we believe He can do so. I've even heard some false teachers say that a failure to dream big is evidence we lack sufficient faith in God, leading to the perverse suggestion that the more outlandish the request, the godlier a person is and the more likely God will be to grant it. Again, this is neither sensible nor biblical.

False teachers use this teaching to attract, excite, and ultimately deceive their audiences so they may manipulate them into making donations. They equate making a large donation to exhibiting "great faith" that leads to great blessing from God (again, *quid pro quo*). The prospect of becoming wealthy simply by asking God to make it so is an irresistible pot of gold at the end of a spiritually bankrupt rainbow.

To support such absurdity, proponents of this heresy will point to scriptures that seem to say when we desire something from God strongly enough and believe He will grant it, He will come through for us. When pressed for biblical support, these false teachers will often cite the following scriptures:

> *Again I say to you, that if two of you agree on earth about anything that they may ask, it shall be done for them by My Father who is in heaven.*
> —Matt. 18:19

> *And all things you ask in prayer, believing, you will receive.*
> —Matt. 21:22

> *And Jesus said to him, "'If You can?' All things are possible to him who believes."*
> —Mark 9:23

> *Therefore I say to you, all things for which you pray and ask, believe that you have received them, and they will be granted you.*
> —Mark 11:24

And so on.

At first glance, these verses may appear to support the conclusion that God stands ready to fulfill our wishes if only we believe He will, but when we take a closer look at each statement made by Jesus, we find the context driving a very different understanding.

In each case, Jesus is speaking of some specific grant by God made in response to our needs. For example, God grants us authority to discipline within the Church (Matt. 18:19), to win souls for the Kingdom (Matt. 21:22, Mark 11:24), or to know that Jesus is truly the Messiah (Mark

9:23). In all cases, such passages are taken out of their proper context to suggest God *always* grants us what we desire under *all* circumstances.

Even a casual Bible student will recognize, however, that such thinking is *not* the general teaching of the Scriptures. We know Jesus told us to pray for God's will to be done, not our own desires, and Jesus even declared that the Father's will be done over Jesus' own will (see Luke 22:42). Jesus' ministry was one of doing the Father's will (i.e., "in the Father's name"), according to John 10:25. If Jesus did the Father's will and not His own, how could we ever expect God to do *our* will?

The key theological flaw in this transactional tenet is the way it ignores God's eternal timetable for the fulfillment of His promises to His children. Transactional theology mistakenly claims God will give us our best life now, but the Bible says our best life comes after our death, in the Kingdom. In fact, for the believer in Jesus Christ, our present life is the *worst* life we will ever know. Instead, we look to our life after death to receive what God has promised.

Perhaps the key passage in the Bible teaching the forward-looking nature of faith is in Hebrews 11, often called the "Hall of Faith":

> *Now faith is the assurance of things hoped for, the conviction of things not seen.*
> —*Heb. 11:1*

> *For by it our ancestors of old gained approval.*
> —*Heb. 11:2*

By faith we understand that the worlds were prepared by the word of God, so that what is seen was not made out of things which are visible.
—**Heb. 11:3**

By faith Abel offered to God a better sacrifice than Cain, through which he obtained the testimony that he was righteous, God testifying about his gifts, and through faith, though he is dead, he still speaks.
—**Heb. 11:4**

By faith Enoch was taken up so that he would not see death; AND HE WAS NOT FOUND BECAUSE GOD TOOK HIM UP; for he obtained the witness that before his being taken up he was pleasing to God.
—**Heb. 11:5**

And without faith it is impossible to please Him, for anyone who comes to God must believe that He is and that He is a rewarder of those who seek Him.
—**Heb. 11:6**

By faith Noah, being warned by God about things not yet seen, in reverence prepared an ark for the salvation of his household, by which he condemned the world, and became an heir of the righteousness which is according to faith.
—**Heb. 11:7**

By faith Abraham, when he was called, obeyed by going out to a place which he was to receive for an inheritance; and he went out, not knowing where he was going.
—**Heb. 11:8**

> *By faith he lived as a stranger in the land of promise, as in a foreign land, dwelling in tents with Isaac and Jacob, fellow heirs of the same promise;*
> —**Heb. 11:9**

> *for he was looking for the city which has foundations, whose architect and builder is God.*
> —**Heb. 11:10**

> *By faith even Sarah herself received ability to conceive, even beyond the proper time of life, since she considered Him faithful who had promised.*
> —**Heb. 11:11**

> *Therefore there was born even of one man, and him as good as dead at that, as many descendants AS THE STARS OF HEAVEN IN NUMBER, AND INNUMERABLE AS THE SAND WHICH IS BY THE SEASHORE.*
> —**Heb. 11:12**

> *All these died in faith, without receiving the promises, but having seen them and having welcomed them from a distance, and having confessed that they were strangers and exiles on the earth.*
> —**Heb. 11:13**

Hebrews 11 defines faith as a confidence that something unseen will eventually come to be reality in our future, which means faith always involves waiting for a future fulfillment, just as Paul says in Romans 8:24: "who hopes for what he already sees?" Therefore, we must understand that God's promises accepted in faith require patient waiting for future fulfillment, after our resurrection. Virtually no promises God makes to believers are fulfilled in this age or in this lifetime.

To prove the point, the writer of Hebrews cites the example of Abraham, who received certain promises from God yet never saw them fulfilled during his earthly lifetime. Abraham believed God would keep His promises after the resurrection, not in his earthly lifetime, which explains why Abraham chose to live as a nomad in Canaan.

Though Abraham was a man accustomed to living in cities in the developed region of Ur, he conspicuously chose to live as a man who owned no land while awaiting the land God promised him after a future resurrection. Abraham was content to forgo the riches of Canaan so he might enjoy the riches of the Kingdom instead *(see Hebrew 11:15-16)*. Abraham's nomadic lifestyle was a testimony to his faith in God's promises and his understanding they would not be fulfilled here.

All true faith should live this way, in anticipation of seeing God's promises fulfilled in eternity, including the promise of receiving eternal life. Our faith in Jesus Christ justifies (i.e., acquits) us before God at the moment we believe, and later it brings a new body and life in the Kingdom. This delayed fulfillment of our promise of salvation is itself a good example of how faith depends on a hopeful expectation of something to come.

The Bible says we are saved (i.e., given eternal life) based on His grace alone, as a gift of God:

> *For the wages of sin is death, but the free gift of God is eternal life in Christ Jesus our Lord.*
> —*Rom. 6:23*

The Christian faith believes the testimony of Scripture concerning Christ, namely that He is the only begotten Son of God, God Himself in the form of a man. Jesus was born a man from a virgin woman, and then He lived a life without sin. Later, He was put to death without cause so that He might take our place in receiving God's judgment for sin, a judgment He Himself didn't deserve. When we believe this testimony, we are showing faith in the promise of God concerning salvation, and by our faith, we receive the promise of eternal life.

We don't receive eternal life on the basis of our own merit or good works, but neither do we receive eternal life in this world. We have received the *promise* of eternal life, and the final fulfillment awaits our resurrected life in the Kingdom. In fact, the Bible even calls our salvation *the promise* of eternal life:

> *This is the promise which He Himself made to us: eternal life.*
> —*1 John 2:25*

Meanwhile, as we await our eternal life, we live in mortal bodies, which must die and be replaced eventually. Christians are not to fear death, precisely because we know we will have eternal life in the age to come *(see Mark 10:30)*. One day when we are resurrected, God's promises of eternal life will be fulfilled, and until then, we walk by faith in that future fulfillment, trusting in the promises of God. We do not see them fulfilled now, because as Paul says:

> *For in hope we have been saved, but hope that is seen is not hope; for who hopes for what they already see?*
> —***Rom. 8:24***

Unfortunately, transactional theology has turned faith on its head by asserting that God's blessings come primarily in this life, and if they fail to materialize, it means we lacked faith. Our lack of faith negated God's opportunity to bless us, they say, so transactional theology maintains we must obtain what our faith expects now or else we didn't possess faith in the first place. This heresy contradicts the biblical definition of faith.

Even worse, transactional theology suggests the believer can determine the content of God's blessings. Rather than rely on God's promises given in Scripture, we're told to trust in our own dreams and God will follow. Believe you will be healed and God will heal you. Believe God will make you rich and He will. This subtle shift moves the focus of our faith from God and His promises to our own desires. When pressed for biblical support for such desires, false teachers twist Scripture like Isaiah 53:5 to suggest God always heals our bodies or Luke 6:38 to claim God rewards our financial gifts with abundant riches. Neither interpretation is correct or consistent with the teaching of the Bible overall, but believers eager to gain what they want readily accept these teachings.

When we believe we will receive what we desire from God, we're believing in our own power to bring us what we want. God is only tangentially involved, fulfilling our orders, while we determine the nature, timing, and degree of that blessing. Once again, it's a *quid pro quo*, transactional relationship that places us in the driver's seat and relegates God to a genie's bottle — and it's complete fiction.

Paul faced a similar heresy in his day, which he addressed in his letter to the Romans:

> *What shall we say then? Are we to continue in sin so that grace may increase? May it never be! How shall we who died to sin still live in it?*
> —***Rom. 6:1-2***

When some in Paul's day suggested that indulging in even greater sin gives God more opportunity to extend His grace, Paul said, "May it never be!" God's ability to grant unlimited forgiveness isn't license for the recipients of His grace to pursue greater sin. On the contrary, God's grace should be cause for us to put sin away, since we understand the great price Jesus paid to bring us God's mercy and forgiveness.

Similarly, God has indeed promised us eternal blessings, but this does not give us license to demand temporal blessings now, and we certainly don't demonstrate greater faith when we place such outrageous demands. On the contrary, we are acting foolishly, without understanding God or His promises. Like those advocating for greater sin so we may give God greater opportunity to demonstrate His mercy, transactional theology advocates placing unreasonable demands on God so He may have opportunity to show His faithfulness to bless us. It's twisted logic intended to exploit and rationalize our greed and lust.

Self-evidently, the clear majority of Christians do not become rich, nor do we receive everything we ask of God — *and this is a good thing*! If we could receive all we desired, we would soon be ruined by the excesses of our lust, and our walk with Christ would be irreparably compromised. Consequently, God is good to deny our requests in many or even most cases. In this way, transactional theology's claims of instant gratification are inevitably shown to be false.

Since transactional theology's claims are so easily disproven by experience (to say nothing of the Bible), why do so many follow its teaching? In a word: *greed*. Any message that promises we can have what we want from God is bound to resonate with our flesh. Even when the promises of riches and health fail to materialize, transactional theology proponents have an answer ready: *it's our fault*.

Tenet #2: We Must First Release God's Favor

The second tenet of transactional theology claims we must "release" God's favor. God wishes to bless us, the false teachers say, but He is unable to bless us unless and until we meet His expectations. In other words, there are *prerequisites* to receiving God's blessings and *grace* (a contradiction in terms), and these false teachers will usually cite examples of biblical characters who demonstrated great faith before receiving great blessings.

This principle of transactional theology provides cover for the failures of the first, because inevitably, transactional theology's promises will fail. God is not a genie, so He doesn't give us everything we desire, and when the promised blessings fail to materialize, we naturally ask what went wrong. The second tenet of transactional theology explains the problem away by claiming we didn't meet God's expectations sufficiently, so God *couldn't* bless us. We didn't show enough faith or "claim" our promise or "speak" our blessing into reality, etc. So, don't blame transactional theology when you don't get what you wanted from God — *blame yourself!*

A favorite example of these teachers (again) is Abraham, who tithed to the priest Melchizedek in Genesis 14. Because of his act of financial faithfulness, false teachers say, Abraham was blessed with great fortune. Therefore, we too will be blessed if we follow in the footsteps of Abraham (i.e., if we give generously to the teacher's ministry). Of course, the false teachers neglect to mention that Abraham neither sought nor expected earthly riches from God. He rested in the promises of God for a future resurrection and Kingdom blessings (as we learned earlier). Moreover, Abraham tithed not as a means of eliciting God's favor but as an act of worship.

Most importantly, the story of Abraham never connects his act of tithing with God's blessings. On the contrary, the Bible says God promised to bless Abraham *before* the man did anything obedient:

> *And I will bless those who bless you, And the one who curses you I will curse. And in you all the families of the earth will be blessed.*
> **—Genesis 12:3**

Since transactional theology eventually disappoints its followers, it needs this second tenet to cover its tracks. This principle allows the false teachers to shift blame away from the teaching itself and onto its followers. It's our fault that God didn't bless us, they say, and we must do more to release God's blessing. Ultimately, those deceived by this nonsense become disillusioned with church, doubtful of God's faithfulness and love, and cynical about their faith. Although the real blame lies with the false claims of transactional theology, victims usually blame themselves or God.

The relationship between the first and second tenets of transactional theology reminds me of the Hans Christian Andersen fable, *The Emperor's New Clothes*. As the story goes, a tailor tricks a king into paying a fortune for a nonexistent set of "invisible" clothing by claiming that only the intelligent may see it. The dim-witted or dishonest cannot see the clothing, the tailor warns the king. Naturally, when the tailor delivers the final product, no one is willing to admit they see nothing, so the king wears it proudly and everyone admires the beautiful outfit. Only after a young boy declares the emperor is wearing no clothes do the villagers come to their senses and confess the truth and their collective vanity.

Similarly, transactional theology is a prosperity fable peddled by con artists who depend upon gullible audiences willing to suspend their disbelief. Most rational people recognize God is not in the business of making His followers rich, yet many would rather play along with the myth out of greed or peer pressure than expose transactional theology as a lie. Although it's obvious churches aren't filled with millionaires and Christians die every day from disease, we nonetheless tell ourselves the claims of heavenly riches and unlimited healing must be true because so many other people believe them. Moreover, if we doubt these claims, we risk disqualification from reward, the teachers say, which ensures everyone stays in line and few are willing to object.

Transactional theology is a clever trap (like the tailor's invisible clothes) that hooks its victims through greed and holds them close through embarrassment or fear. As a result, followers of transactional theology behave like addicted gamblers desperately hoping the *next* pull of the heavenly lever will produce a big payoff. They will continue giving their money to the charlatans ("sowing a seed," as they say) hoping it will release God's favor by proving they possess the necessary faith. Like the hapless emperor, few will ever admit they have been fooled until they are broke or broken.

If only we would read our Bible! Peter warned the Church that this deception would arrive one day:

> *Many will follow their sensuality, and because of them the way of the truth will be maligned; and in their greed they will exploit you with false words; their judgment from long ago is not idle, and their destruction is not asleep.*
> —***2 Pet. 2:2–3***

Scripture declares that the transactional theology "emperor" has no clothes. Our desires are usually self-centered and short-sighted, and therefore, a loving God often should and will reject our requests. In place of our desires, the Lord gives our heart new, godly desires *(see Psalm 37:4)*, and He chooses the manner and timing of those blessings.

The first and primary blessing we receive from God is eternal life through our faith in Jesus Christ. We received this blessing without any requirement of obedience and solely as a matter of God's grace *(see Ephesians 2:8-9)*. Moreover, our faith alone has made us fellow heirs with Christ, meaning we have also received an eternal inheritance, which awaits us in the Kingdom age. We did nothing to receive the blessings of the New Covenant, and we did nothing to be included in Christ's inheritance. Though we may experience the Lord's discipline from time to time, our relationship with Him was established and is sustained by His grace alone and not through a series of transactions, as Paul testifies:

> *In Him, you also, after listening to the message of truth, the gospel of your salvation — having also believed, you were sealed in Him with the Holy Spirit of promise, who is given as a pledge of our inheritance, with a view to the redemption of God's own possession, to the praise of His glory.*
> —***Eph. 1:13–14***

Beyond our salvation, the Lord also grants us our rewards, which also await in the Kingdom, not in this life, as Scripture says:

> *Blessed be the God and Father of our Lord Jesus Christ, who has blessed us with every spiritual blessing in the heavenly places in Christ.*
> —***Eph. 1:3***

> *Do not store up for yourselves treasures on earth, where moth and rust destroy, and where thieves break in and steal. But store up for yourselves treasures in heaven, where neither moth nor rust destroys, and where thieves do not break in or steal.*
> —***Matt. 6:19-20***

These passages and others like them disprove transactional theology's claims and expose the enemy's true motive. Satan is working through this heresy to take a believer's attention off the eternal and fix it on the fallen world, which is Satan's dominion. When we seek this world's rewards rather than waiting for our reward in the Kingdom, we become tempted by every manner of sin while losing interest in sacrificial service to Christ. As John tells us:

> *Do not love the world nor the things in the world. If anyone loves the world, the love of the Father is not in him. For all that is in the world, the lust of the flesh and the lust of the eyes and the boastful pride of life, is not from the Father,*

but is from the world. The world is passing away, and also its lusts; but the one who does the will of God lives forever.
—1 John 2:15-17

If God's greatest blessing for us, our eternal life, came because of His grace alone and not by our works, then why should we believe lesser blessings are dependent on our performance? Why would God freely hand out His greatest blessing to us yet place demands upon us before granting us other blessings? This is illogical and further exposes the fallacy of a *quid pro quo* relationship with God.

How Did this False Teaching Gain its Audience?

Millions of people around the world (believers and unbelievers alike) remain committed to a *quid pro quo* view of God even though the Bible clearly teaches otherwise. Why? Because the Church is suffering from widespread biblical illiteracy.

George Barna, the founder of a market research firm specializing in American religious beliefs, routinely conducts surveys of evangelical Christians, and his findings are disheartening:[3]

- Based on a 2018 survey, adults who use the Bible daily account for just 14% of the total adult population.[4]

- Only a third of self-identified Christians can identify a biblical spiritual gift they claim to possess.[5]
- Less than one out of every five born again adults (19%) has a biblical worldview.[6]
- Only half of all self-identified Christians firmly believe that the Bible is completely accurate in the principles it teaches.[7]
- Barely one-quarter of adults (27%) are confident that Satan exists, and even fewer believe a person can be influenced by angels or demons.[8]
- An overwhelming majority of self-identified Christians (81%) contend that spiritual maturity is achieved by following rules (i.e., legalism). (Barna Group, 2009)[9]

Research like Barna's confirms that biblical illiteracy is a real and growing threat to orthodox Christian belief and practice. Without leaders committed to teaching God's Word in a methodical fashion, believers cannot move beyond an immature and easily manipulated understanding of their relationship with Christ. Believers need the meat of God's Word, but many pastors in churches today offer little more than porridge for the mind — or as the writer of Hebrews puts it, milk (Heb. 5:13). False doctrines like transactional theology find an easy footing in such an environment.

While milk (i.e., simple truths of the Bible) may be appropriate for Christians in their first days of walking with

Jesus, we're eventually called to graduate to more challenging truths found in God's Word ("solid food," according to Heb. 5:12). Understanding the Bible in a deep way is our primary spiritual defense against false teaching *(see Heb. 5:14)*, but when established Christians are likewise ignorant of biblical truth, who will come alongside new believers to disciple and protect them from false teaching? This is how unbiblical teaching like transactional theology gains a perch in the church: *because few know the Bible.*

As the Apostle Paul approached the end of his life, he recognized that his earthly ministry was about to conclude. So, he wrote a letter to his apprentice, Timothy, with words of advice that are equally true for us today:

> *I solemnly charge you in the presence of God and of Christ Jesus, who is to judge the living and the dead, and by His appearing and His kingdom: preach the Word; be ready in season and out of season; reprove, rebuke, exhort, with great patience and instruction. For the time will come when they will not endure sound doctrine; but wanting to have their ears tickled, they will accumulate for themselves teachers in accordance to their own desires, and will turn away their ears from the truth and will turn aside to myths.*
> —***2 Tim. 4:1-4***

Paul told Timothy to preach the Word, specifically to reprove, rebuke, and exhort the body of Christ with great patience and instruction. Paul gave his charge because he said a time would come when believers would rather have their ears tickled with pleasing words than be challenged to understand and obey proper Bible teaching. The church, Paul foretold, would come to prefer false teachers who affirmed their fleshly desires (e.g., the pursuit of riches, power, and pleasure) over true teachers who reminded the Church of its obligations to Christ.

Paul's words were prophetically speaking of our day. Today, churches worldwide are filled with believers following false teachers who say pleasing things like, "God will grant our wishes when we ask Him." Their audiences generally will not demand biblical support for their teachers' outlandish claims, nor would they be capable of discerning whether the Scriptures were being applied properly in any case. Biblical illiteracy has rendered the church ripe for deception and incapable of defending the truth.

The widespread problem of biblical illiteracy in the Church means the average believer is condemned to repeating the sin of Adam in the Garden. When faced with the enemy's temptations to sin, we substitute our thoughts for God's Word, which gives us license to act according to our desires by calling it obedience to God. Simply put, biblical ignorance allows our pride and lust to lead us into foolishness and sin.

Everyone who has raised children knows that good parenting means not giving a child everything he or she desires (assuming we have the child's best interests at heart). Good parents only allow children to have what's best for them, so why would we expect our perfect Father in heaven to do otherwise for us? Why would a loving God abdicate His responsibility to shepherd us and guide our choices by allowing our sinful hearts to dictate what we receive? Obviously, He wouldn't, yet this is exactly the teaching of transactional theology.

Biblically illiterate Christians are persuaded to believe that God can be their personal genie, whom they can call upon to accomplish their desires. The Gospels give us an interesting example of such bad thinking at work in the life of a major biblical character: Mary, the mother of Jesus. Consider Mary's request of Jesus in Cana.

> *On the third day, there was a wedding in Cana of Galilee, and the mother of Jesus was there; and both Jesus and His disciples were invited to the wedding.*
>
> *When the wine ran out, the mother of Jesus said to Him, "They have no wine."*
>
> *And Jesus said to her, "Woman, what does that have to do with us? My hour has not yet come."*
>
> *His mother said to the servants, "Whatever He says to you, do it."*
>
> *Now there were six stone waterpots set there for the Jewish custom of purification, containing twenty or thirty gallons each. Jesus said to them, "Fill the waterpots with water." So they filled them up to the brim. And He said to them, "Draw some out now and take it to the headwaiter." So they took it to him.*
>
> *When the headwaiter tasted the water which had become wine, and did not know where it came from (but the servants who had drawn the water knew), the headwaiter called the bridegroom, and said to him, "Everyone serves the good wine first, and when the people have drunk freely, then he serves the poorer wine; but you have kept the good wine until now."*
>
> **—John 2:1–10**

Weddings were important in the Jewish tradition, and whole towns were often invited to attend. The hosts, typically the groom's parents, usually invested a great deal in the event both socially and financially. If the wedding went badly and the guests weren't happy, then custom permitted them to take back their wedding gift, so the wedding host had a lot on the line!

During the wedding, Mary noticed the wine was running low. Wedding hosts were expected to provide a lavish banquet for their invited guests, and wine was the drink of the day. Wine was symbolic of joy, so running out of wine would be a terrible embarrassment for the host. Probably out of empathy for the host's circumstances, Mary turned to Jesus and informed Him of the situation.

Interestingly, Mary initially made no request of Jesus. By Jesus' response, however, we can see Mary expected Him to correct the problem, probably through a supernatural act of some kind.

Of course, Mary didn't need to spell it out for Jesus, since Jesus knew Mary's thoughts. In response, Jesus asks Mary in John 2:4:

> *Woman, what does this have to do with us? My hour has not yet come.*

By addressing His earthly mother as "woman," Jesus wasn't being disrespectful or rude to Mary. Woman was the name of the first female, the wife of Adam, so Jesus' use of the term intimated His position as Mary's Creator, which served to remind her of her place. Secondly, Jesus' statement that His time has not yet come was a mild rebuke reminding Mary that His supernatural powers were intended to further the will of His Father, not to serve Mary's personal interests.

Everything Jesus did while on earth was perfectly aligned with the will of the Father, as Jesus Himself said:

> *Therefore Jesus answered and was saying to them, "Truly, truly, I say to you, the Son can do nothing of Himself, unless it is something He sees the Father doing; for whatever the Father does, these things the Son also does in like manner.*
> *—John 5:19*

So, had Jesus done anything outside the Father's will — even an act of kindness like the one Mary suggested — it would have disqualified Jesus as our perfect sacrifice and rendered Jesus' earthly ministry void. Notice in John 2:4 when Jesus asks Mary, "What does this have to do with us?" He uses a plural pronoun ("us"). Most people assume this refers to Jesus and Mary, but I believe it refers to Jesus and the Father. Jesus is asking what this moment has to do with the ministry Jesus and the Father are at work to accomplish on earth.

The answer to that question is "nothing." Mary's concerns for the host's reputation were honorable, but Jesus says they were not aligned with the Father's will. Mary viewed Jesus' power as a tool to serve her (noble) interests, and as a result, she unwittingly adopted a transactional mindset. In response, Jesus cautioned Mary, "My hour has not yet come," meaning the appointed time by the Father for Jesus to reveal Himself publicly as Messiah had not yet arrived.

Based on Jesus' response, I assume Mary had been hoping to kill two birds with one stone with her request of Jesus. Perhaps she hoped to persuade Jesus to correct the wedding *faux pas* while at the same time propelling Him into the limelight with this miracle so He could reveal Himself as Messiah. This wasn't the time for Jesus to be revealed, yet Mary believed the wedding in Cana was the right time for Him to go public *because it was the right time for her.* Mary was wrong to dictate the timing of God's plan for Jesus, because only the Father could determine the timing and manner of His Son's unveiling.

After Jesus' rebuke, Mary said nothing. She simply turned to the servants and instructed them to do whatever Jesus told them. Mary seemed confident Jesus would do as she requested despite His objections, and surprisingly, Jesus acquiesced to her demands. He directed the servants to serve water from the washing jugs, which had now turned to wine.

Why did Jesus comply with Mary's request after having just corrected her? Jesus was threading the needle by honoring His earthly mother and obeying His Heavenly Father without contradiction. First, Jesus was keeping the commandment to honor His mother by fulfilling her request to address the need for more wine. Jesus obeyed His mother by performing His first miracle at this event, turning water into wine.

Nevertheless, Jesus also obeyed His Father by accomplishing the miracle in a quiet way so that only the servants at the wedding knew what had taken place. Only

60 years later, when John wrote His Gospel, did the world first learn of this miracle! Jesus fulfilled Mary's desire to spare her host embarrassment while simultaneously obeying the Father's will to remain hidden for that time.

This story is a powerful example of how we sometimes bring requests or expectations to the Lord that don't align perfectly with His desire or timing or purpose, yet in those situations, God may still grant our requests, at least in part, for His own purposes. When this happens, we cannot conclude that we dictated the outcome or that God does our bidding. Jesus was not doing all that Mary expected; He only did that which agreed with the Father's will.

When the Lord grants us a request, we know our request was in agreement with God's will, though in many cases, we will receive only part of what we requested or may receive it in surprising ways. In Mary's case, she received part of what she desired (e.g., the wine), but the Lord did not allow her to reveal His identity prematurely through the miracle. For that, she received a rebuke for her wrong motives.

If Mary could stumble in this way, then it's no surprise many believers today are doing so. In fact, I believe this account of Mary in Cana has been preserved in Scripture as a lesson for all believers about the dangers of misusing Jesus' authority or overestimating our role in our relationship with Him. We do not have the power to determine outcomes in God's plan, we cannot dictate the terms of our blessings, and we are not in control of God's timing. We are His servants, not the other way around.

Transactional theology trains Christians to think in opposite ways by insinuating we hold the reins for our own future: we control God's responses by what we say to Him or do for Him, and through our prayer life, we can influence God's priorities, much like Mary tried to influence Jesus.

When we think and act this way, we should expect negative results, as James warns:

> *You lust and do not have; so you commit murder. You are envious and cannot obtain; so you fight and quarrel. You do not have because you do not ask. You ask and do not receive, because you ask with wrong motives, so that you may spend it on your pleasures.*
> —*James 4:2-3*

The Church must declare war on transactional theology and on any teaching that suggests a *quid pro quo* relationship with God. The Bible declares God does His will and does not cater to our lusts. As with Mary at the wedding in Cana, the Lord may occasionally give us what we ask — but only because it serves His eternal purposes, and even then, He may rebuke us for selfish motives.

The key to defeating transactional theology is to reestablish an appreciation of God's sovereignty in the minds of believers, and to do that, we must address biblical illiteracy in the Church. People plan their ways, but the Lord directs our steps (Proverbs 16:9), so believers must appreciate the first rule of following God: remembering who leads and who follows (hint: we do the following).

This book is an attempt to further that defeat by teaching Christians what the Bible says about the sovereignty of God, beginning with how we make requests of God in the first place. Since we know the Lord will only do His will, what is the purpose of prayer?

CHAPTER TWO

Quid Pro Quo Prayer?

If a Christian can be fooled into believing God is a genie, it will be easy to convince him or her that our prayers can control God's will. Many Christians assume prayer is a tool for influencing God, which suggests we can influence or even change God's mind with our prayers. Naturally, believers who view prayer in this way will be confused when told God's mind cannot be changed (as we shall soon see), so they may wonder: why bother praying?

Before we can answer that question, we must first establish a biblical understanding of prayer. The Bible commands believers to pray for our needs and desires:

> *Be anxious for nothing, but in everything by prayer and supplication with thanksgiving let your requests be made known to God.*
> **—Philippians 4:6**

> *...pray without ceasing...*
> **—1 Thess. 5:17**

> *Therefore, confess your sins to one another, and pray for one another so that you may be healed. The effective prayer of a righteous person can accomplish much.*
> *—James 5:16*

Making requests of God is obviously biblical, and those requests are often for personal desires and needs. All prayer starts there, but in Jesus' model of prayer in the "Our Father," He also taught us to desire that the Father's will be done.

Similarly, when Jesus prayed the night before He died on the cross, He said:

> *Father, if You are willing, remove this cup from Me; yet not My will, but Yours be done.*
> *—Luke 22:42*

So, while the Bible does ask us to bring our requests before the Lord, it also teaches that our desires must be secondary to God's desires for us. In other words, Jesus tells us to pray, "Lord, please give me what I want, unless what You want for me is something else, in which case do what you prefer." In effect, Jesus is teaching us that the purpose of prayer is to change *our* minds, not to change God's mind, because the first is necessary and the second is impossible.

Scripture assures us God never changes His mind. For example, in Numbers 22–23, a Jewish prophet Balaam is hired by one of Israel's enemies, the Moabite king Balak, to curse the nation of Israel, but God will not allow a prophet to curse his own people. Since it was God's will that Balaam bless Israel, every time Balaam opened his mouth to curse Israel, he uttered blessings instead. Neither King Balak nor the prophet Balaam could carry out his own plan, because they were acting against the will of God.

At one point, as the prophet Balaam tried to act against God's wishes by cursing the nation of Israel, the Lord caused the following words to come from Balaam's mouth:

> *God is not a human, that He should lie, nor a human being, that He should change His mind. Does He speak and then not act? Does He promise and not fulfill?*
> **—Num. 23:19**

Ironically, God used the disobedient prophet's own mouth to confirm to the prophet that he could not have his way with God. Though the prophet had asked God repeatedly through prayer for the opportunity to curse Israel, the answer always came back "no." God's will must be done, and as God Himself said, He will not change His mind concerning what is good and necessary. No amount of pleading will lead God to do our will over His own will, because if He did our will, it would be sin for God.

A second story from the Old Testament confirms this truth. In the book of First Samuel, the prophet tells King Saul he cannot expect God to change His plans to suit Saul's desires:

> *Also the Glory of Israel will not lie or change His mind; for He is not a human that He should change His mind.*
> —*1 Sam. 15:29*

Samuel told King Saul he had forfeited his throne to David. Naturally, Saul didn't like this outcome, so he pressed God to change His mind. In response, the prophet Samuel informed King Saul that God cannot change His mind. What God has determined must happen, since God has decreed it. Therefore, we pray for God's will to be done; there is no other option. Praying for God to do something other than His will is literally asking God to do the impossible.

Moreover, there can never be a good reason for God to change His mind, because He already considered every possibility before the foundation of Creation and chose the best option. We have no new information to offer God. We have no argument He hasn't already considered. It is impossible for God to change His mind, because He already arrived at the perfect plan, and therefore any deviation from that plan would arrive at something less than perfect, which is sin.

To illustrate the difference between how God thinks and how we think, imagine a friend promises to paint your house for free. You're pleased by the offer and eagerly await the fulfillment of that promise. A few weeks go by, but your friend never returns to paint your house. Naturally, you begin to doubt he will keep his promise. Your friend never mentioned a specific date when he would accomplish the job; nevertheless, the passing of time leads us to question whether it will ever happen.

We wonder what caused our friend to break his promise. Perhaps circumstances changed to prevent your friend from painting your house. Perhaps he got sick. Perhaps he moved away. Perhaps he forgot. Whatever the reason, the passage of time leads you to conclude that he changed his mind.

The passage of time *can* change human thoughts and plans, because we don't know the future, and therefore we can't take future events into account when we make plans. But God exists outside time, and in fact, He is the author of all history. Since God exists equally in the past, present, and future, He can anticipate everything and anything, so He only makes promises He can keep. There is nothing He will learn tomorrow that He doesn't already know today. He has already considered every piece of data available in the universe, and because everything is under His control, there is no force or cause in the universe that could lead God to act or think differently tomorrow than He did yesterday.

The theological principle that captures this truth is the immutability of God. *Immutable* means unable to change, so we understand from Scripture that God is unchanging in His character, will, and purpose. Simply said, it's impossible for God to change His mind (or anything else) for any reason, because He is in all ways perfect as He is.

The Father also knows what we want before we ask Him in prayer, so even if it were possible for God to learn or move to some new perspective (which it isn't), He isn't gaining that new information from us. He already knows everything we could ever know. Remember Christ's words regarding prayer:

> *And when you are praying, do not use meaningless repetition as the Gentiles do, for they suppose that they will be heard for their many words. "So do not be like them; for your Father knows what you need before you ask Him."*
> **—Matt. 6:7–8**

Before we ever begin to pray, God knows what we are going to ask Him and even the specific words we will use in making our requests. Therefore, nothing we say will persuade Him to change. So, what is the purpose in praying to a sovereign God who cannot be changed by our prayers?

In the book of Genesis, we find a story of Abraham and Sarah entertaining three traveling strangers, who bring them great news that within the year, Sarah will bear a son, Isaac. At first, Abraham didn't recognize his visitors, but as they finished eating, Abraham became aware that he was in the presence of the Lord. Genesis 18 reveals this moment:

> *Then the men rose up from there and looked down toward Sodom; and Abraham was walking with them to send them off. The LORD said, "Shall I hide from Abraham what I am about to do, since Abraham will surely become a great and mighty nation, and in him all the nations of the earth will be blessed?*
>
> *"For I have chosen him, so that he may command his children and his household after him to keep the way of the LORD by doing righteousness and justice, so that the LORD may bring upon Abraham what He has spoken about him."*
>
> *And the LORD said, "The outcry of Sodom and Gomorrah is indeed great, and their sin is exceedingly grave.*

"I will go down now, and see if they have done entirely according to its outcry, which has come to Me; and if not, I will know."

Then the men turned away from there and went toward Sodom, while Abraham was still standing before the LORD.
—Gen. 18:16–22

Scripture reveals God's silent thought, "Shall I hide from Abraham what I am about to do?" as the three figures get up to depart. Though phrased as a question, this is actually a statement — a rhetorical question. God was speaking to Abraham's heart to provoke his interest in these angels' plans. The Lord was declaring, "I will not hide from Abraham what I'm about to do."

Earlier in Genesis, God found Abraham (Abram at the time) living in Ur and called him to move to Canaan and live as a nomad, determined to remain apart from the godless culture surrounding him. God instructed Abraham to leave behind his family and travel only with his wife, Sarah (Sarai). Instead, Abram elected to bring his nephew, Lot, whose father had died.

God's wisdom in commanding Abraham to leave family behind became evident when Lot and Abraham settled in Canaan. Lot was a difficult person who made life hard for Abraham. His herds competed with Abraham's livestock for the limited pasture, so Abraham and Lot eventually parted ways. Abraham gave Lot first pick of the land, and Lot chose to settle near Sodom. Lot eventually moved inside the city, while Abraham continued living nomadically.

Returning to Genesis 18, we find God ready to judge the wickedness of Sodom, but before He acts, the Lord asks rhetorically, "Shall I hide from Abraham what I am about to do?" God's plan to judge Sodom is already fixed. He has firmly resolved that Sodom will be judged — it must be. His character requires justice, and His holy purpose intends to make Sodom an example for all time:

> ...and if He condemned the cities of Sodom and Gomorrah to destruction by reducing them to ashes, having made them an example to those who would live ungodly lives thereafter...
> —*2 Pet. 2:6*

Christians often forget God is constantly at work in our world just as He was in Abraham's day. He reveals His work to His children and invites us to join Him in that work. Each time we seize the opportunity, we will be trained in righteousness by the Father, which is why the Lord reveals His plans to us in the first place. This was the situation for Abraham as well.

The Lord wanted to include Abraham in His work of preparing Canaan to become Israel, as part of the promise He'd made to Abraham to create and bless many nations through him. For this reason, God intended to judge Sodom, and He included Abraham in that work. The Lord required Abraham be a man who stood as an example to all future generations, walking in His ways and raising his children to do the same. The Lord wished to teach Abraham about His mercy and His judgment, and Sodom and Gomorrah were to be that opportunity — which required that the Lord reveal His plans to Abraham in the hope it would invite him into the work through prayer.

Consider a parent who works on his car in the garage. On one occasion, the parent extends an invitation to his child to help. If the child is disinterested or distracted, he or she loses the chance to learn from their parent. The parent still goes about the work without the child, and the work still gets done, but the child misses the opportunity to experience the joy of working with the parent.

On the other hand, if the child seizes the moment and joins in the work, he or she is blessed to spend time working with the parent. The relationship is strengthened, and knowledge is shared. Meanwhile, the parent is prepared for the job to take longer because the child is involved. The parent anticipates more mistakes will be made. When the parent asks for a wrench, the child selects a screwdriver. Nevertheless, the parent tolerates the difficulty because the relationship matters more.

In fact, it makes no logical sense for a parent to include the child in the process of fixing a car if the parent's only goal is fixing the car, but it makes perfect sense if the parent's goal is training the child. Our Heavenly Father does the same thing with us as He did with Abraham in Genesis 18.

In the passage from Genesis, God announces to Abraham that He plans to visit Sodom to determine whether it is as sinful as He has heard. Of course, God already knew the truth about Sodom, so He spoke these words for Abraham's benefit, and God knew how His words would influence Abraham. Abraham knew the city would be destroyed, and rightly so, and he also knew his nephew, Lot, would be caught up in the judgment. The city's reputation was so bad, the news had reached all the way to heaven, so certainly it would have reached Abraham only a few miles away. Even today, we use the term "Sodom and Gomorrah" to describe an incredibly sinful place.

So, having heard God's plans, and out of concern for his nephew, Abraham responded with one of the most dramatic examples of intercessory prayer in the Bible. Abraham petitioned God to save Lot, and his prayer offers one of the clearest pictures anywhere in the Bible of how prayer works, while demonstrating the purpose of prayer in light of a sovereign God:

> *Abraham came near and said, "Will You indeed sweep away the righteous with the wicked? Suppose there are fifty righteous within the city; will You indeed sweep it away and not spare the place for the sake of the fifty righteous who are in it? Far be it from You to do such a thing, to slay the righteous with the wicked, so that the righteous and the wicked are treated alike. Far be it from You! Shall not the Judge of all the earth deal justly?"*
>
> *So the LORD said, "If I find in Sodom fifty righteous within the city, then I will spare the whole place on their account."*
>
> *And Abraham replied, "Now behold, I have ventured to speak to the Lord, although I am but dust and ashes. Suppose the fifty righteous are lacking five, will You destroy the whole city because of five?"*
>
> *And He said, "I will not destroy it if I find forty-five there."*
>
> *He spoke to Him yet again and said, "Suppose forty are found there?"*
>
> *And He said, "I will not do it on account of the forty."*
>
> *Then he said, "Oh may the Lord not be angry, and I shall*

speak; suppose thirty are found there?"

And He said, "I will not do it if I find thirty there."

And he said, "Now behold, I have ventured to speak to the Lord; suppose twenty are found there?"

And He said, "I will not destroy it on account of the twenty."

Then he said, "Oh may the Lord not be angry, and I shall speak only this once; suppose ten are found there?"

And He said, "I will not destroy it on account of the ten."

*As soon as He had finished speaking to Abraham the L*ORD *departed, and Abraham returned to his place.*
—**Gen. 18:23–33**

Abraham appears to have been quite the negotiator. He began engaging with the Lord by appealing to God's character and nature. God cannot act against His holy and perfect nature, so if we should ask Him to do so, that prayer is guaranteed to fall on deaf ears. Abraham, on the other hand, appealed to God's perfect mercy and justice when he asked God if He would destroy the wicked and the righteous. Abraham knew the answer was no, God would preserve the righteous and judge the unrighteous, because this was consistent with God's perfect character, as Peter tells us:

> *...and if He condemned the cities of Sodom and Gomorrah to destruction by reducing them to ashes, having made them an example to those who would live ungodly lives thereafter; and if He rescued righteous Lot, oppressed by the sensual conduct of unprincipled people (for by what he saw and heard that righteous man, while living among them, felt his righteous soul tormented day after day by*

> *their lawless deeds), then the Lord knows how to rescue the godly from temptation, and to keep the unrighteous under punishment for the day of judgment...*
> —*2 Pet. 2:6–9*

Abraham smartly began his negotiation by reminding God of His righteous character, and then asked God to spare the city for the sake of the righteous. Abraham's goal was to save his nephew, and he had assumed that to save Lot, he must convince God to save the entire city.

So, Abraham made a calculated gamble. Abraham didn't know whether Lot was counted among the righteous of Sodom, and if Lot wasn't righteous (i.e., believing), then Abraham knew he would perish. At the same time, Abraham assumed God might agree to spare the whole city if enough righteous called it home. Abraham quickly estimated that fifty righteous people might be found in the depraved city of Sodom, and he petitioned God to spare the whole city for their sake.

The Lord agreed to this proposal, and perhaps because He agreed so quickly, Abraham began to rethink his proposal. Abraham wondered if perhaps he overestimated, so he began lowering his bid first to 45, then to 40, then 30, then 20, and finally 10. Abraham's concern here wasn't for the city as a whole; his concern was for Lot and his family. Since he couldn't know whether Lot was righteous, however, he was bargaining for the whole city.

As Peter wrote earlier, the Lord is perfectly discriminating. He holds the unrighteous accountable and rescues the righteous, but in this case, the Lord was willing to withhold judgment for a time to encourage Abraham. Remember, the point of this encounter was to encourage Abraham to join in God's work, which is to rescue the righteous and punish the unrighteous. Abraham was participating in this work through his intercession, though he wasn't fully aware at first.

The question we need to consider is: did Abraham change God's mind through this process? According to Peter, the Lord's will is to punish the wicked and rescue the righteous. Abraham was asking the Lord to spare the entire city of wicked people for the sake of a few righteous, and the Lord agreed. At first that would seem as though the Lord's intentions were changed by Abraham's petition, but we could say the same for Mary in Cana. When she walked away from Jesus, she left thinking Jesus was going to make more wine and expose Himself as Messiah. In the end, she got the wine but not the exposure, because Jesus could only do the Father's will. So, what did Abraham get?

Abraham lobbied for God to spare Sodom for the sake of ten righteous, hoping this was enough to ensure his nephew survived. Interestingly, Abraham stopped asking before the Lord stopped agreeing, so we will never know whether he could have bargained for even fewer. Still, ten righteous people seemed like a good gamble even for a city as depraved as Sodom, so the bargaining ended there.

Following Abraham's intercession, the angels traveled to Sodom and entered the city, where they found exactly what they expected to find: depravity so great that the city's destruction was assured. Only Lot's family was righteous, which fell far short of the ten required to save the city. The angels removed Lot and his family from the city before destroying it in fire and brimstone.

We wonder: did Abraham's prayer work? Abraham prayed God would save the city if He found ten righteous people, and since He found only four, the city was destroyed. God kept His bargain with Abraham. However, what Abraham really wanted was for God to save Lot and his family, though Abraham never specifically asked God for their safety. I believe Abraham never named Lot in his prayers because he was unsure whether Lot was believing and Abraham knew better than to ask God to spare the unrighteous. Instead, Abraham tried to save Lot indirectly by bargaining for the entire city.

God knows what we want (and need) before we ask, so even when we don't know what to ask or when we ask for the wrong thing, the Lord still works for our good. As Peter taught us in his letter, God's character required Him to save Lot and his family, regardless of whether Abraham asked for that (the Lord's will be done!). Likewise, God's justice required that the unrighteous city be destroyed, and He agreed to Abraham's terms knowing the city did not have ten righteous. He allowed Abraham to set the terms so Abraham could participate in the work of God, yet God did not allow Abraham's involvement to alter His plan.

In the end, God's will for Sodom and for Lot was done just as God planned. Sodom was destroyed along with all the wicked, and the righteous members of Lot's family were rescued from the destruction, just as Peter explained. At the same time, He invited Abraham into His work so Abraham could learn and grow in his understanding of God through the encounter. During the process, Abraham perceived he was influencing God's choices and actions, but in reality, God never actually changed His plans. In fact, God was already at work carrying out His plan even as Abraham was petitioning God.

Remember the two angels who went into the city? They came in the likeness of men, so each had two human hands. That details tells us God knew He would only need to rescue four righteous who were reluctant to leave, with each needing a hand to pull them to safety. God knew how many He needed to save even as He was entertaining Abraham's bargaining. So, God accomplished His precise will for Sodom and nothing more, for that is all God can do.

At the same time, God also gave Abraham everything he asked for and everything he wanted. Abraham asked for the city to be saved if enough righteous could be found, but since that number wasn't found, the city was destroyed. God kept the bargain, yet He also saved Lot and his family, which was all Abraham really wanted in the first place. As with the wedding in Cana, God did only what His will desired, but He worked in a way that encouraged His servant Abraham to be part of the work. God orchestrated the circumstances to ensure Abraham could participate and learn even as God achieved His will. That's the purpose of prayer: that we might join God in His work while learning through the process. We participate in the only way we know — by interceding for what we desire — but in the end, God's will be done.

We can imagine this story turning out a different way. Had Abraham prayed for God to spare the city unconditionally, then we know Abraham would not have seen his prayer answered successfully because God would have had to deny His character to grant it. God *must* judge unrighteousness because that is the righteous response to sin. So, Abraham's situation was much like Mary's. He requested something he couldn't have, but he received what was in keeping with God's will.

When we examine the many verses in Scripture regarding prayer, we find a common theme: we are instructed to pray in faith and seek the will of God.

> *Whatever you ask in My name, which will I do, so that the Father may be glorified in the Son. If you ask Me anything in My name, I will do it.*
> —*John 14:13-14*

In ancient Far Eastern culture, making a request in another person's name meant you were representing that person with full authority to speak on his or her behalf. To speak in someone's name required you to know them well and to have received specific direction on how to speak, as if you were the person. Naturally, anything you said would be honored just as if the person you represented spoke it.

In that sense, if we ask something in Jesus' name, we are acting on His behalf with His blessing and authority. The phrase "in Jesus' name" doesn't have magical power, and we can't add it to a prayer to guarantee a positive answer from God. It simply reflects our desire to pray in Jesus' will, as if we were speaking for Him. Clearly, if we are not speaking as He would speak, then our prayer is not according to His will.

We remember that the model Jesus gave us for prayer in Matthew 6 began, "Our Father, Who is in Heaven, hallowed be Your name" (Matt. 6:9). Those are declarative statements. They are not requests. There are no requests in the "Our Father" prayer until the second half, when Jesus tells us to ask for His "kingdom come, Your will be done on earth as it is in Heaven," and to "give us this day our daily bread," etc. So, Jesus taught us to begin prayer by making declarative statements that remind us who is in charge. In a sense, Jesus was setting our expectations for how prayer works: we can ask for anything, but we must expect God's will to be done!

In fact, every aspect of our life on earth, including our prayer life, is supposed to be directed at doing God's will just as Jesus did. As we seek His will, we will offer prayers, and to the extent those prayers are acceptably within His will, they will be answered affirmatively. As we observe which prayers are answered affirmatively and which are denied, we learn to discern His will. The child who asks his or her mom for candy at the grocery store shortly before dinner quickly learns that this request receives a no, but a request for fruit yields a yes. Likewise, we ask God for many things, and over time we learn what pleases God's heart by noticing what He approves and what He doesn't.

The key lesson in all this is, we have no power to change God but we do have the opportunity join God in His work. That is a very great thing indeed and far better than changing God. If we could change God's mind, we would make God less God by making Him more like us. On the other hand, when we work with God to do His will, we become more like Him over time, which the Bible calls sanctification. This is the power of praying to a sovereign God who has ordained a great plan for us, and He knows what we need even before we ask. God decides the work and ultimately accomplishes the work, and He invites us to join Him through our prayers. To Him be the glory!

CHAPTER THREE

Give and Get Prosperity

The modern Church (like all modern society) has become obsessed by the pursuit of wealth and health. Most mainstream Christian teaching seems focused on these topics, and some pastors preach almost nothing *except* messaging on how believers obtain wealth and prosperity. The Church's current obsession with wealth is not hard to understand (who doesn't lust after riches?), nor is it new. The desire for wealth is universal, as are teachers willing to preach about it. Perhaps that's why Christ spent more time addressing the topic of money in the Gospels than virtually any other subject.

When we consult Jesus' teaching on the topic, what do we find? Did Jesus tell us to focus our spiritual attention on obtaining earthly prosperity? Did Christ say His mission was making His followers rich in this life? In fact, do we believe that Jesus came to earth to live as a Man and die on a cross merely to guarantee us earthly prosperity? If that were His goal, couldn't Jesus have dropped some manna from heaven into our laps and avoided the trouble of the incarnation (to say nothing of His crucifixion)? The notion that Jesus cares about our earthly prosperity is denied by His own teaching on the matter. Jesus sums up His teaching on materialism this way:

> *Do not worry then, saying, "What will we eat?" or "What will we drink?" or "What will we wear for clothing?" For the Gentiles eagerly seek all these things; and your Heavenly Father knows that you need all these things. But seek first His kingdom and His righteousness, and all these things will be added to you.*
> —*Matt. 6:33*

Jesus clearly didn't want the church to make the pursuit of wealth a personal goal, yet verses like this one are rarely quoted by transactional theology proponents, especially not by those who teach the prosperity heresy.

The prosperity heresy, or "prosperity gospel," claims that God promises material blessings and physical wellbeing to all believers. Believers "release" these blessings by "sowing a seed" (i.e., donating to a ministry), which results in God returning that donation many times over. This teaching is both heretical and self-evidently nonsensical, since we see no evidence of believers becoming wealthy by giving. Giving to the needs of the saints is clearly biblical and expected in Scripture *(see 2 Cor. 8–10)*, but there is no promise that such obedience will result in a financial windfall for the believer.

Nevertheless, false teachers push this message relentlessly, hoping to manipulate our greed to line their pockets. They promise we can be rich if we donate to their ministry, but it's easy to recognize the *quid pro quo* theology in such teaching. They tell us give to God and He will give to us, but in truth the only person who becomes rich under prosperity teaching is the prosperity teacher. Meanwhile, the fleeced flocks become increasingly disillusioned and angry at God for not fulfilling His "promises."

How do these false teachers persuade so many into believing transactional theology? They strut across the stage wearing expensive designer clothing and fancy jewelry while making conspicuous references to their country club lifestyle and private jets. They hold themselves up as models of God's willingness to make believers rich if we adopt a *quid pro quo* approach to our faith. The same God who made them rich will do the same for us if we make a donation, they claim, but we know where those fancy suits and luxury jets *really* came from: fleecing the sheep!

This obvious con game would be laughable if it weren't so dangerous. The prosperity gospel heresy is a man-centered message that diminishes God's sovereignty, distorts and contradicts His word, and encourages our lustful desires. A true, biblical perspective of prosperity, on the other hand, maintains an appreciation for God's sovereignty over wealth, beginning with an acknowledgment that God owns everything:

> *The earth is the* Lord's, *and all it contains, the world, and those who dwell in it.*
> —*Ps. 24:1*

Since God owns (and therefore controls) all wealth on earth, He determines how much each person on earth will receive. The rich do not become rich merely because of talent or hard work, nor are the poor suffering for their own incompetence or laziness. We understand God decides who will be rich and poor. Obviously, our intelligence and hard work will play a role in how God blesses us, but that just reflects the way God carried out His eternal purpose. At the end of the day, we cannot explain our station in life purely on the basis of human ability or effort. The Bible says God is in control of these outcomes.

Consider Scripture's testimony:

> *The LORD makes poor and rich; He brings low, He also exalts.*
> —*1 Sam. 2:7*

> *The rich and the poor have a common bond, the LORD is the maker of them all.*
> —*Prov. 22:2*

Scripture says the world has rich and poor, and the Lord is the One who makes both. Knowing that God is sovereign over wealth, Christians are called to put aside a pursuit of earthly riches to pursue godliness and the Kingdom instead. Likewise, we are called to give generously to the needs of the saints knowing that the Lord is our supply.

Even as we do works of charity, we understand we're not "paying it forward," as some teach, because we do not have a *quid pro quo* relationship with God. He does not owe us anything for our service to Him:

> *Which of you, having a slave plowing or tending sheep, will say to him when he has come in from the field, "Come immediately and sit down to eat"? But will he not say to him, "Prepare something for me to eat, and properly clothe yourself and serve me while I eat and drink; and afterward you may eat and drink"? He does not thank the slave because he did the things which were commanded, does he?*
>
> *So you too, when you do all the things which are commanded you, say, "We are unworthy slaves; we have done only that which we ought to have done."*
> —**Luke 17:7–10**

Because our funds belong to God (He gave them to us!), when He asks us to dispose of them in ways that glorify Him, we have every reason to obey. In this way, giving is like prayer: we do not give for God's benefit in receiving, but for our benefit in obeying.

Moreover, if God is in control over all earthly resources and He assigns them to people according to His own purposes, then we have reason to be content with His allotment to us. Clearly, what we have financially was what God determined would be best for us. Teaching others that riches are a sign of God's approval denies His sovereign decision to make some richer than others.

Instead of making our lives a stressful pursuit of wealth, we should obey Christ's call to seek first righteousness, which means using our time to serve the cause of the Kingdom program. Seeking righteousness first means prioritizing spiritual success over material success. Obviously, we still have earthly needs, so we must still spend at least some time on material pursuits, but that effort is balanced by knowing God sovereignly determines our financial station in life.

The Bible has a word for accepting the financial station God has assigned to us: contentment. Finding contentment in whatever circumstances God has assigned doesn't mean we can't advance in life or build personal wealth, but it does mean we shouldn't make those things our primary goal in life. Contentment allows a Christian to run the rat race at a slower pace, to cease striving for the highest rung on the corporate ladder, to stop trying to keep up with the Joneses.

The writer of Hebrews says contentment is a sign of our trust in the Father:

> *Make sure that your character is free from the love of money, being content with what you have; for He Himself has said, "I WILL NEVER DESERT YOU, NOR WILL I EVER FORSAKE YOU"...*
> —*Heb. 13:5*

Trusting God for what we need brings contentment by silencing that inner voice demanding we get more in life. Contentment gives us the confidence to step back from the incessant drive for success and material comforts so we can focus on the more important goals in life: namely, pleasing Christ. Christians who lack contentment never find that peaceful "centeredness" in life, and as a result, they are forever tempted to set aside Kingdom goals in order to pursue worldly gain, in keeping with the parable Jesus taught in Luke 8:

> *The seed which fell among the thorns, these are the ones who have heard, and as they go on their way they are choked with worries and riches and pleasures of this life, and bring no fruit to maturity.*
>
> *—Luke 8:14*

We only have so much time and so many resources, and Jesus says if we squander them in pursuit of the "riches and pleasures of this life," we forgo opportunity to produce spiritual fruit that leads to eternal reward.

Paul also warned us about this danger in 1 Timothy:

> *If anyone advocates a different doctrine and does not agree with sound words, those of our Lord Jesus Christ, and with the doctrine conforming to godliness, they are conceited and understand nothing; they have a morbid interest in controversial questions and disputes about words, out of which arise envy, strife, abusive language, evil suspicions, and constant friction between people of depraved mind and deprived of the truth, they suppose that godliness is a means to financial gain.*
>
> *But godliness is actually a means of great gain when accompanied by contentment. For we have brought nothing into the world, so we cannot take anything out of it either.*
>
> *If we have food and covering, with these we shall be content.*
>
> *But those who want to get rich fall into temptation and a snare and into many foolish and harmful desires which plunge people into ruin and destruction. For the love of*

> money is a root of all sorts of evil, and some by longing for it have wandered away from the faith and pierced themselves with many griefs. But flee from these things, you person of God, and pursue righteousness, godliness, faith, love, perseverance, and gentleness.
>
> —*1 Timothy 6:3-11*

Paul described those who teach the prosperity gospel (and other false gospels) as men and women who use godliness as a means of gain. They are depraved and deprived of the truth, Paul says, and they deceive many who are likewise devoid of the truth.

On the other hand, Paul adds, godliness can be a means of great gain *if* accompanied by contentment. In other words, we can gain great wealth through our pursuit of Christ so long as we are content with whatever Christ provides for us in this life. By being content with what we have now, we find the self-discipline to crucify our flesh and serve Christ, confident that our eternal rewards will be more than enough compensation.

The Bible does promise blessing for obedience to Christ, and those blessings may include earthly rewards, but true earthly rewards are rarely material. More often, we are rewarded with respectful children, a loving husband or wife, good health, or a long life. At the same time, the Lord promises to bless us with eternal material rewards, which Christ describes in numerous places, including Matthew 6:

> Do not store up for yourselves treasures on earth, where moth and rust destroy, and where thieves break in and steal. But store up for yourselves treasures in Heaven,

where neither moth nor rust destroys, and where thieves do not break in or steal; for where your treasure is, there your heart will be also.
—**Matt. 6:19-21**

This is the "great gain" Paul tells us is available for those who combine godliness with contentment. Paul is saying, when we pursue godliness, we please Christ, and in response, Christ rewards us with heavenly gain. We are not saved by our works, of course, but Paul is teaching us we are rewarded for them in the Kingdom.

Christians are often surprised to learn that the Bible encourages all Christians to pursue heavenly rewards through good works. Our reward is not salvation itself. The Bible calls our salvation a free gift, not a reward or prize to be earned. Nevertheless, after having received eternal life through faith in Jesus, believers may then serve Jesus for the opportunity for reward, as Paul explains:

Therefore, we also have as our ambition, whether at home or absent, to be pleasing to Him. For we must all appear before the judgment seat of Christ, so that each one may be recompensed for his deeds in the body, according to what he has done, whether good or bad.
—**2 Cor. 5:9-10**

Every Christian will stand before Christ for a judgment after resurrection, and at that moment, our earthly service to Jesus is evaluated and good service is recompensed, or rewarded. This is the Judgment Seat of Christ, the moment when believers learn how much treasure in heaven we have stored up.

Remember, Jesus told us we can only pursue one love at a time, whether God or money, so if we spend our life on earth pursuing earthly riches, we will not be able to serve Jesus. On the other hand, if we live a contented life satisfied with what we already have, we will have time and opportunity to serve Christ. Then, in serving Him well, we become rich in heaven, and heavenly rewards are far better than any earthly rewards, as Paul says:

> *But just as it is written, "Things which eye has not seen and ear has not heard, and which have not entered the heart of man, all that God has prepared for those who love Him."*
> *—1 Cor. 2:9*

Jesus has better things prepared for us in the Kingdom than we can provide for ourselves here, so there is no point in trying to make this world "heaven" by amassing great wealth. Nothing we accumulate here can compare to what God has waiting for us after our resurrection, so in that sense, contentment is the means to true riches, as the Bible says.

Does this mean a Christian who possesses significant wealth is sinning? Not at all. Wealth is a tool, and like any tool, it can be put to great use by God when stewarded by a wise and prudent servant. The Bible never condemns the possession of riches, only the love of riches (1 Tim. 6:10), and a poor believer is not automatically more pleasing to Christ than a wealthy believer. Often, poverty tempts believers into greater love for money. Once more, the best attitude toward wealth is contentment. Do not long for what you lack, strive for more than you need, or place your trust in what you have. As Solomon said:

> *Keep deception and lies far from me, give me neither poverty nor riches; Feed me with the food that is my portion, that I not be full and deny You and say, "Who is the LORD?" Or that I not be in want and steal, and profane the name of my God.*
> —*Prov. 30:8-9*

So, if the Lord chooses to bless you with great financial resources in this life, recognize the accompanying responsibility. Don't become devoted to riches, turning them into a curse, or become careless in the management of your resources and waste the opportunity they offer you to serve Christ. Recognize the Lord gives wealth to use for the good of the Kingdom.

On the other hand, should the Lord choose to give you less wealth than you desire (and isn't that true for most of us?), accept His sovereign choice and do not allow the pursuit of wealth to overtake more important life goals, like serving Jesus. Instead, devote that effort to building up treasure in heaven.

Christ gave us a powerful lesson in storing up treasure in heaven in the Parable of the Unrighteous Steward. This parable is considered by many to be the most difficult parable in the all the Bible. If that's true, it's because the concepts it teaches about wealth are so foreign to what the world tells us and from what we're hearing in churches everywhere we turn today. It turns transactional theology, and particularly the prosperity gospel, on its head. Jesus teaches this parable in Luke 16:

> Now He was also saying to the disciples, "There was a rich man who had a manager, and this manager was reported to him as squandering his possessions. And he called him and said to him, 'What is this I hear about you? Give an accounting of your management, for you can no longer be manager.'
>
> "The manager said to himself, 'What shall I do, since my master is taking the management away from me? I am not strong enough to dig; I am ashamed to beg. I know what I shall do, so that when I am removed from the management people will welcome me into their homes.'
>
> "And he summoned each one of his master's debtors, and he began saying to the first, 'How much do you owe my master?'
>
> "And he said, 'A hundred measures of oil.'
>
> And he said to him, 'Take your bill, and sit down quickly and write fifty.'
>
> "Then he said to another, 'And how much do you owe?'
>
> And he said, 'A hundred measures of wheat.'
>
> He said to him, 'Take your bill, and write eighty.'
>
> "And his master praised the unrighteous manager because he had acted shrewdly; for the people of this age are more shrewd in relation to their own kind than the people of light. And I say to you, make friends for yourselves by means of the wealth of unrighteousness, so that when it fails, they will receive you into the eternal dwellings. Whoever is faithful in a very little thing is faithful also in much; and whoever who is unrighteous in a very little thing is unrighteous also in much. Therefore, if you have not been faithful in the use of unrighteous wealth, who will entrust

the true riches to you? And if you have not been faithful in the use of that which is another's, who will give you that which is your own?"
—**Luke 16:1–12**

The difficulties in interpreting this parable are immediately apparent. In the parable, a master is ready to fire his manager for mismanagement. After being informed of his fate, the steward appears to double down on his mismanagement by cheating the manager. When the master learns about the steward's action, he praises him for his shrewdness, and Jesus applauds the steward's actions as well. Jesus ends the parable asking His disciples to imitate the steward. Why do the manager and Jesus approve of this scoundrel's behavior, much less invite believers to imitate him?

Some historical context will help to shine light on these matters. In Jewish culture, wealthy business owners often employed managers to handle their business affairs. These managers would attend to every detail of the master's business, including purchasing and selling goods and collecting payment from customers. Occasionally, customers lacked the funds to pay the full price for goods or services, so they would seek credit terms from the manager.

Since the Law (e.g., Exodus 22:25, Leviticus 25:36-37, Deuteronomy 23:19) prohibited a Jew from charging another Jew interest, it became customary for managers to set a higher price for the goods or services (as much as double the normal price) in exchange for extended payment terms. When the bill was finally repaid, the manager could keep the extra amount for himself as compensation for having assumed the risk of delayed payment.

Given that background, we can now see why the manager in the parable was praised. As the manager learns he will be fired for mismanagement, he considers his future. This manager knows he was a hard man who made many enemies during his years in service to his master. Now that he's facing unemployment and will soon be dependent on the kindness of others, he devises a shrewd plan to ensure a soft landing. He remembers that the debts currently owed to his master were doubled to include his fee, yet he will never be able to collect those funds. That future income is worthless, since he won't be employed by the master on the day those bills are repaid.

So the manager decides to turn this useless wealth into an advantage. He quickly runs to each of his master's debtors and reduces their debts *by the amount of his fee*, leaving only the amount owed to the master. In some cases, the bill is cut by 20%, and in other cases, it's cut in half! In reducing the bill, the manager eliminates future income he never would have received anyway, and in the process, he builds goodwill with these merchants. Later, when he is unemployed and comes back seeking their help, the manager hopes these clients will look favorably upon him.

Jesus praises this manager's actions as shrewd because he traded something of no value (i.e., his master's uncollected debts) for something of great worth (i.e., goodwill among potential future employers). Not only was this good for the manager, but it was also good for the master and his customers. The manager gained the favor of the master's clients, the clients saved money, and the master's reputation was enhanced.

At the end of the parable above, Christ makes a comparison between the "sons of this age" (i.e., all unbelievers) and the sons of light (i.e., all believers) using the phrase "in relation to their own kind." Jesus is saying believers could learn a thing or two about handling wealth by watching how unbelievers deal with one another in the area of finance. Like the manager in the parable, believers should recognize that wealth is a tool, and it should be used to maximum spiritual advantage. Use it well and it can bring great spiritual benefits, but use it foolishly and you miss eternal opportunities.

In Luke 16:9 Jesus says believers should use the wealth of unrighteousness to make friends for the sake of eternity. The wealth of unrighteousness is Jesus' term for the money of this world, the currency of this unrighteous planet. Jesus calls the money of this world "unrighteous" wealth to distinguish it from the wealth of the future Kingdom, and the key difference is that unrighteous wealth stays here while Kingdom wealth travels with us. We all die and leave our earthly wealth behind, and eventually the world and everything in it will be destroyed.

What if we could turn that unrighteous wealth we leave behind into lasting treasure in heaven? Like the manager, we would be turning something worthless into something of future value. Jesus says if we follow the manager's shrewd example, we can do just that! Jesus says to use your earthly wealth to bless other believers now; then, when we see each other in the heavenly realm, they will welcome us into eternal dwellings. Simply put, we will remember who was generous now, and we will carry that appreciation into the Kingdom age. Moreover, the Lord Himself will note our generosity and reward us for it in the Kingdom.

Whether you use your earthly resources to fund worldwide ministries reaching new believers, to support your local church ministries, or to help a believing widow buy groceries, you are using the wealth of unrighteousness to make eternal friends and earn eternal benefits. This is a shrewd use of your wealth, because you are turning perishable wealth into eternal wealth. You are making something of limited value into something of infinite value. This mature Christian perspective on wealth recognizes that God promises to bless us in eternity, not necessarily here and now.

In fact, we quickly come to the opposite conclusion. Collecting and storing up earthly wealth is foolish when you consider the alternatives. Rather than store it up, we should put earthly wealth to work for eternity. If we see earthly wealth as our reward, then we miss the opportunity. The person who earns $10,000 and spends it all on serving Christ will be far richer in eternity than the one who earns $1,000,0000 and dies with all of it in the bank. Our eternal life is in the Kingdom, and our life here is temporary, so we should use this life to prepare for the next. Any departure from this perspective leads to loss, as Jesus taught:

> Then He said to them, "Beware, and be on your guard against every form of greed; for not even when one has an abundance does their life consist of their possessions."

> *And He told them a parable, saying, "The land of a rich man was very productive. And he began reasoning to himself, saying, 'What shall I do, since I have no place to store my crops?'"*
>
> *"Then he said, 'This is what I will do: I will tear down my barns and build larger ones, and there I will store all my grain and my goods. And I will say to my soul, "Soul, you have many goods laid up for many years to come; take your ease, eat, drink and be merry."'*
>
> *"But God said to him, 'You fool! This very night your soul is required of you; and now who will own what you have prepared?' So are those who store up treasure for themselves and are not rich toward God."*
>
> —**Luke 12:15-21**

We are called to be rich toward God, not toward ourselves, which means not making our goal the accumulation or storing of earthly wealth. The prosperity gospel turns this biblical teaching upside down by encouraging a desire for earthly wealth. This false teaching says God intends to make us rich (thus legitimizing our lust for wealth) and the wealthier we are now, the more God approves us. This teaching is the complete opposite of the truth (i.e., a lie) and has Satan's fingerprints all over it. We must turn away from any such teaching that encourages us to repeat the mistake of the rich man with the barns full of grain.

In place of this dangerous teaching, we need to learn to trust God for our provision, accepting His will for us and prioritizing Kingdom goals over earthly goals. Wealth is a test of our hearts, and our faithful use of earthly wealth reveals how trustworthy we will be with eternal riches, Jesus says in Luke 16. We pass this test when we live with eyes for eternity, accepting that treasure is best stored in heaven.

CHAPTER FOUR

Limitless Healing

An elderly man attending a faith healing service one night was surprised when the preacher suddenly yelled at him from the stage saying, "Stand up and walk!" The old man was caught off guard by the preacher's command, but slowly he proceeded to stand up from his wheelchair, and then with assistance from an usher, he took a few steps toward the stage. The amazed crowd clapped and yelled in praise. Then the preacher asked the old man, "So, how do your legs feel now?"

The old man replied, "My legs are fine, but I still can't see."

No doubt you've heard of "faith healers," those charismatic stage performers who claim to have the gift of supernatural healing. Typically, they reserve their healing work for special settings (think: tent revivals) where loud music, bright lights, and a circus-like atmosphere conspire to fool the audience. Dramatic, instant "healings" are staged to convince a crowd hungry for a spectacle. The healings ultimately serve as the setup for arm-twisting financial appeals.

These shows are a con game and another *quid pro quo* lie. The scam centers promise healing for those who have "faith," and if faith is lacking, then the healing can't happen. This is another form of transactional theology, and like the rest, it is a house of cards.

First, a true spiritual gift (including the gift of healing) never depends on the faith of the person *receiving* the service of that gift. For example, a teacher with the gift of teaching doesn't depend on the "faith" of his or her students to be able to teach. The gift of teaching operates regardless of the state of the hearts of those receiving the teaching. The gifted teacher offers just as much biblical insight to those of little of no faith as to those of great faith.

Similarly, the gift of leadership doesn't require faith in those who are being led, nor does the gift of service require faith in those being served. A true spiritual gift operates according to the power and will of God, and God can perform a healing in anyone at any time. False teachers commonly link their healing powers to a person's faith to give excuse when their promises of healing fail, so they can encourage greater financial gifts as "proof" of faith.

In reality, faith healers are usually capable of doing no more than make the blind walk and the lame see. Faith healers like to promise us God *always* heals the believer, provided we show enough faith (another *quid pro quo* message). Like the prosperity heresy, this lie is easy to expose: self-evidently, we all die sooner or later. Sooner or later, our body fails us, as God intended, so clearly God doesn't heal us every time. For that reason, faith healers rely on the same excuse to explain away their inability to perform a healing: if you didn't get healed, you didn't have enough faith.

Given the similarities between the prosperity heresy and fake faith healers, it comes as no surprise that the antidote is also the same. The end of any transactional thinking is always a proper appreciation of God's sovereignty. God is sovereign over the health of our bodies, and the course of our life is determined according to God's sovereign plan. Any illnesses or injury we may experience is according to God's will, and even the length of our life is determined by God, according to the Bible.

> *Humans, who are born of woman, are short-lived and full of turmoil. Like a flower they come forth and wither. They also flee like a shadow and do not remain. You also open Your eyes on them and bring them into judgment with Yourself. Who can make the clean out of the unclean? No one! Since a person's days are determined, the number of their months is with You; and their limits You have set so that they cannot pass.*
> **—Job 14:1–5**

Job testifies here that God isn't merely aware of our future — He authored it! God has numbered a person's days, meaning He has *determined* how many days we will live on earth, and Job says He will not allow us to pass that limit. The more carefully we consider this truth, the more radically it will change the way we live our life.

Consider how much time, money, and effort we spend trying to lengthen our days. Yet God says our plans don't change a thing! Even those who don't believe the Bible must agree that no one lives forever, so self-evidently, we are fighting a losing battle. Plastic surgery, cosmetics, vitamins, and exercise may change our appearance or improve our health for a time, but they can't add one day to their lives, according to the Bible.

> *And who of you by being worried can add a single hour to your life?"*
> —***Matt. 6:27***

If limitless healing is a logical impossibility and contrary to Scripture, how do false teachers find an audience in the church for their message? I believe the answer is the fear of death. Unsaved humanity lives with an ever-present fear of death, but believers have no reason to be controlled by such fear. Scripture teaches we have been freed from the penalty of sin and, therefore, from the fear of death:

> *Therefore, since the children share in flesh and blood, He Himself likewise also partook of the same, that through death He might render powerless him who had the power of death, that is, the devil, and might free those who through fear of death were subject to slavery all their lives.*
> —***Heb. 2:14–15***

The writer says Christ took on flesh and blood to suffer death in our place and to pay the price for sin, and when God raised Jesus from the dead, He demonstrated death was no longer our enemy. By our faith in Jesus, we will be resurrected also, and the future reality of our bodily resurrection removes Satan's power to control us through our fear of death. Simply put, we no longer have reason to fear death, so we are free to make decisions without regard for when we may die.

Since Christians have been freed from fear of death, we no longer have reason to prioritize avoiding death over more important priorities like serving Christ; nor should be become preoccupied with miraculous healing, since we know our eternal destiny is a new body. Nevertheless, we all suffer the pains of aging and poor health from time to time, and when we do, we also hope for healing. False faith healers know this, too, and they lure our desire for healing away from the eternal and back to the temporal. Instead of the promises of resurrection and a new eternal body, false faith healers stir up a renewed fear of death inside believers, preoccupying us with worries about how long we live or how healthy our body can be.

As long as we fear death, Satan can use that fear to control us again. False teachers prey on fear of illness, weakness, and death to control their followers. They tailor their appeals to those frightened of dying, and they offer miracle cures of "faith" for those who do their bidding. Paul warned us a time would come when believers would follow after those who told them what they wanted to hear:

> *For the time will come when they will not endure sound doctrine; but wanting to have their ears tickled, they will accumulate for themselves teachers in accordance to their own desires, and will turn away their ears from the truth and will turn aside to myths.*
> *—2 Tim. 4:3–4*

Of course, the fact that false faith healers operate in the Church doesn't mean genuine healing is not also at work today, and the gift of healing operates in the same way as any other spiritual gift. This means the gift functions according to the will and power of the Holy Spirit, and it operates in ways consistent with Scripture. Just as a believer with the gift to teach can't always interpret Scripture correctly, neither can a believer with the gift of healing cure every ailment. Every spiritual gift depends entirely on the will of God, so healing happens only if it is within God's will.

Scripture gives no assurance that the Lord will always heal our bodies on request. On the contrary, sooner or later, our body must die and return to dust — unless we live until the resurrection day. On that day, we will receive a new eternal body, but until then, our physical bodies march toward death. Therefore, we cannot say God always heals; otherwise, no Christian would ever die! Instead, we must acknowledge that the Lord may heal us if He desires, but eventually, He stops healing us so we might graduate to the next body. This is not a problem to be solved but a blessing, since we should desire the arrival of our new, sinless and eternal body far more than the continuation of our corrupt body.

Sadly, well-meaning pastors and teachers have been deceived by the success of false healers and prosperity teachers and have begun to repeat their teachings. The Church must put a stop to this descent into apostasy. We must find the courage of Hezekiah, who removed the high places, broke down the sacred pillars, and cut down the Asherah poles (2 Kings 18).

Christians should not obsess over our health out of fear of impending death, though that doesn't mean we may be careless with our health. Scripture tells us to treat our bodies with reverence:

> *Flee immorality. Every other sin that a person commits is outside the body, but the immoral person sins against their own body. Or do you not know that your body is a temple of the Holy Spirit who is in you, whom you have from God, and that you are not your own? For you have been bought with a price: therefore, glorify God in your body.*
> —*1 Cor. 6:18-20*

> *Even so consider yourselves to be dead to sin, but alive to God in Christ Jesus. Therefore do not let sin reign in your mortal body so that you obey its lusts, and do not go on presenting the members of your body to sin as instruments of unrighteousness; but present yourselves to God as those alive from the dead, and your members as instruments of righteousness to God.*
> —*Rom. 6:11-13*

We find similar guidance in 1 Corinthians 3 and 2 Corinthians 6, instructing us to treat our body with care since it is the temple of God. Paul instructs us to flee sins involving physical acts of immorality because the Holy Spirit indwells us and therefore owns our body. When we use our body for immoral purposes, we essentially bring the Holy Spirit with us into our sin and make Him a witness to our depravity. Treating our bodies with reverence is about revering the Spirit within us, not our flesh.

On the one hand, these verses are telling Christians to make the preservation of our physical body a priority. On the other hand, Paul declares that he looks forward to the replacement of his present body:

> *For indeed in this house we groan, longing to be clothed with our dwelling from heaven, inasmuch as we, having put it on, will not be found naked. For indeed while we are in this tent, we groan, being burdened, because we do not want to be unclothed but to be clothed, so that what is mortal will be swallowed up by life.*
> —*2 Cor. 5:2–4*

Paul says here Christians "groan" while living in our present "house" and "tent" (i.e., our earthly body), because we long for our new body instead. No Christian should desire living one day longer than necessary in our present body of sin knowing a body of glory awaits. Obviously, we don't invite or hasten our death, but neither should we live in fear of death. False teachers are experts at exploiting fear of death, primarily by convincing us God is prepared to heal us every time we ask provided we do what's required to gain His favor (another *quid pro quo* lie).

The truth is, God is sovereign over the length of our life and He has already appointed the day of our death, according to Job 14. So, why waste time and energy working in vain to extend our lives beyond the limit God set? Instead, let's set our mind on eternal things, while living each day in ways that glorify Him.

What would it look like to devote our bodies in service to God without concern for the length of our lives? I believe the Apostle Paul gives us that example. Jesus assigned Paul a vitally important ministry for the early Church, and if any man could rightly prioritize long life, it would have been the most successful evangelist the Church has ever known. Consider how many people Paul might have converted and taught had he been able to live 100 years or longer!

Paul's importance to the early church can't be overstated, yet according to the record of Acts, Paul never placed much priority on maintaining good health or avoiding risks in the course of his ministry. In fact, Paul lived a difficult and dangerous life. He found nearly every conceivable way to put his body in harm's way, subjecting it to misery, wearing it down, and undermining its health. Paul did so for the sake of the Church, the Kingdom, and the glory of God. He entered into circumstances knowing he would be stoned, beaten, jailed, scourged, and worse, because he knew this was how he was called to glorify Christ.

Imagine if Paul had decided it would be safer for him to remain in Ephesus rather than embark on the long and difficult journey to Macedonia. What if he had decided to preserve his strength instead of risking his life to reach Corinth? How would we remember the Apostle if he had preferred the safety of Antioch over the trials of Thessalonica or Derbe? If Paul had adopted the transactional theological view that places a priority on the health of our current body, he probably wouldn't have made those journeys, considering them too dangerous.

Thankfully, Paul knew his reward would be found in heaven and God was sovereign over his earthly life. He learned to take poor health in stride as a natural consequence of life and ministry:

> *Because of the surpassing greatness of the revelations, for this reason, to keep me from exalting myself, there was given me a thorn in the flesh, a messenger of Satan to torment me — to keep me from exalting myself!*
>
> *Concerning this I implored the Lord three times that it might leave me. And He has said to me, "My grace is sufficient for you, for power is perfected in weakness." Most gladly, therefore, I will rather boast about my weaknesses, so that the power of Christ may dwell in me. Therefore, I am well content with weaknesses, with insults, with distresses, with persecutions, with difficulties, for Christ's sake; for when I am weak, then I am strong.*
> —*2 Cor. 12:7–10*

> *For we do not preach ourselves but Christ Jesus as Lord, and ourselves as your bondservants for Jesus's sake. For God, who said, "Light shall shine out of darkness," is the One who has shone in our hearts to give the Light of the knowledge of the glory of God in the face of Christ. But we have this treasure in earthen vessels, so that the surpassing greatness of the power will be of God and not from ourselves; we are afflicted in every way, but not crushed; perplexed, but not despairing; persecuted, but not forsaken; struck down, but not destroyed; always carrying about in the body the dying of Jesus, so that the life of Jesus also may be manifested in our body. For we who live are constantly being delivered over to death for Jesus's sake, so that the life of Jesus also may be manifested in our mortal flesh. So death works in us, but life in you.*
> —*2 Cor. 4:5–12*

Paul says his earthly body was constantly suffering for the sake of ministry. Speaking of himself and the other

Apostles, Paul says they were afflicted, perplexed, persecuted, and struck down, but these afflictions could not defeat them because their afflictions had a good purpose in God's economy. Those afflictions were intended to weaken the body so that the strength of Christ living in the apostles would shine through.

Paul says his body was just an earthen vessel. In Paul's time, lamps were often made from crude, translucent clay pots whose only value was in what they held. Some were used to hold oil that burned as a candle, and the light of the flame would shine through the translucent pottery. Paul compares the believer's body to such a vessel, in the sense that our body's value is found in what it contains: the light and life of Christ living in us. The weaker our earthen vessel becomes, the stronger the light shines forth and gains attention, Paul is saying.

Paul goes on to say that Satan was not the one afflicting the Apostles; Satan doesn't have that power, and he certainly doesn't want to glorify Christ through our affliction. The Greek grammar in 2 Corinthians makes clear that the same One who is working to glorify Christ is the One who afflicted the Apostles. This One is the Holy Spirit Himself. So, God subjects believers to these afflictions, not for the purpose of destroying us, but to ensure our weakness is always evident and Christ's strength is always visible.

Paul's challenging teaching is summed up in one paradoxical statement: "death works in us, but life in you." Paul says that the more obediently he ministered to the Corinthian church, the more he suffered physically at the hands of his enemies who opposed the gospel. This was "death" working in Paul, in the sense that Paul placed himself in harm's way for the sake of the gospel. Nevertheless, the more Paul suffered for Corinth, the more the Corinthian believers grew in their faith as they witnessed Paul's perseverance and selfless faith. This was "life" working in the Corinthian church as a result of Paul's suffering.

For that reason, Paul says he didn't regret the abuse his body took or the trouble he caused the local church in attracting new enemies. These trials were necessary to bring God the glory and grow the church. More importantly, Paul accepted it was God's plan for him to suffer in the work of the ministry:

> *For all things are for your sakes, so that the grace which is spreading to more and more people may cause the giving of thanks to abound to the glory of God. Therefore, we do not lose heart, but though outwardly we are decaying, yet inwardly we are being renewed day by day. For momentary, light affliction is producing for us an eternal weight of glory far beyond all comparison, while we look not at the things which are seen, but at the things which are not seen; for the things which are seen are temporal, but the things which are not seen are eternal.*
> *—2 Cor. 4:15-18*

Paul knew experiencing physical trials would be a necessary part of his ministry, because he didn't want to convert people into being followers of Paul. He wanted to convert people into believers in Jesus Christ, which meant Paul's personal strength couldn't compete with God's glory. If Paul's ministry results drew attention to his physical health, he would have diminished the glory of God and misled the Church about where Paul's success originated.

Anyone inclined to believe that God stands ready to grant all believers wealth and health must also believe that Paul and the other apostles were horrible role models who lacked faith to "release" God's favor. Clearly, this is not true, as Scripture itself testifies:

> *Remember those who led you, who spoke the Word of God to you; and considering the result of their conduct, imitate their faith.*
> —**Heb. 13:7**

The Bible testifies that the Apostles' words and life were exemplary, and they serve to expose transactional theology's lies. Paul's life in particular demonstrated that blessing for the believer comes from making sacrifices and enduring trials. As Paul notes in 2 Corinthians 4:17, any affliction we experience in this life is light and momentary (from the view of eternity), but the eternal rewards that follow will be weighty and permanent. Long after our money has been left to others and our body has turned to dust, we will still be enjoying the heavenly treasure and eternal, sinless body God has prepared for us.

Speaking of eternal treasure, did you know every believer's service to Christ will be tested at the Judgment Seat of Christ (2 Cor. 5:10)? After we die, we will give an account of what we did to serve Jesus in faith, and we will be rewarded in the Kingdom based on that testimony. How will you answer Christ in that moment? What will your testimony be on that day? Are you living to serve Christ or yourself?

Those who buy into transactional theology will likely enter their judgment moment unprepared, because if you believe rewards are found in this life (e.g., earthly prosperity, health, etc.), then you're unlikely to put much thought into pleasing Christ for eternal reward. Transactional theology turns the biblical view of service and reward on its head by proposing that God will serve us with treasure now, to our pleasure, while the Bible says we serve God, to His pleasure, for reward in heaven.

> *Whatever you do, do your work heartily, as for the Lord rather than for men, knowing that from the Lord you will receive the reward of the inheritance. It is the Lord Christ whom you serve.*
> —*Col. 3:23-24*

The prosperity gospel heresy and other transactional lies emphasize this world and all it contains, which limits our eternal perspective and leads us to prioritize our desires over Christ's. The Scriptures, on the other hand, emphasize the importance of making sacrifices in this life for the sake of the Kingdom and the glory of God, knowing God will provide for our needs and reward us in the Kingdom.

We would all do well to adopt the psalmist's perspective:

Hear this, all peoples; give ear, all inhabitants of the world,

Both low and high, rich and poor together.

My mouth will speak wisdom, and the meditation of my heart will be understanding.

I will incline my ear to a proverb; I will express my riddle on the harp.

Why should I fear in days of adversity, when the iniquity of my foes surrounds me,

Even those who trust in their wealth and boast in the abundance of their riches?

No one can by any means redeem the live of another or give to God a ransom for them — For the redemption of a soul is costly, and they should cease trying forever — That they should live on eternally, that they should not undergo decay.

For one sees that even those who are wise die; the stupid and the senseless alike perish and leave their wealth to others.

Their inner thought is that their houses are forever and their dwelling places to all generations; they have called their lands after their own names.

But people in their pomp will not endure; they are like the beasts that perish.

This is the way of those who are foolish, and of those after them who approve their words. Selah.

As sheep they are appointed for Sheol; death shall be their shepherd; and the upright shall rule over them in the morning, and their form shall be for Sheol to consume so that they have no habitation.

But God will redeem my soul from the power of Sheol, for He will receive me. Selah.

Do not be afraid when someone becomes rich, when the glory of their house is increased; For when they die they will carry nothing away; His glory will not descend after them.

Though while they live they congratulate themselves — And though people praise them when they do well for themselves — They shall go to the generations before them; they will never see the light.

—Ps. 49

CHAPTER FIVE

Human-Centered Evangelism

The Bible calls all Christians to build the Body of Christ through evangelism, the process of sharing the good news of Jesus Christ with the world. Most Christians are familiar with the "Great Commission" found at the end of Matthew's Gospel, and these well-known verses offer important details on why and how we evangelize. Let's take a close look at the specific wording:

> *And Jesus came up and spoke to them, saying, All authority has been given to Me in Heaven and on earth. Go therefore and make disciples of all the nations, baptizing them in the name of the Father and the Son and the Holy Spirit, teaching them to observe all that I commanded you; and lo, I am with you always, even to the end of the age.*
> *—Matt. 28:18–20*

These words deserve our careful consideration. Jesus says all authority in heaven and on earth has been given to Him, which implies no One else has the power to save men and women from their sin. For that reason, Jesus says, "Go therefore." In other words, because we know Jesus has all authority and He is the only solution to the problem of sin, we can confidently go to the world with that message as He commands us, knowing we will not go in vain. Our obedience to go *will* bring a measure of success, because the One sending us is also the One with authority to save the men and women we meet.

Paul instructed the Corinthian church on this principle when he wrote:

> *For when one says, "I am of Paul," and another, "I am of Apollos," are you not mere humans? What then is Apollos? And what is Paul? Servants through whom you believed, even as the Lord gave opportunity to each one. Paul planted, Apollos watered, but God was causing the growth. So then neither the one who plants nor the one who waters is anything, but God who causes the growth. Now the one who plants and the one who waters are one; but each will receive their own reward according to their own labor. For we are God's fellow workers; you are God's field, God's building.*
> —*1 Cor. 3:4–9*

When we evangelize, we "sow" the Word of God, planting seeds in the hearts of people. When a seed takes root to bring new faith, we cannot take credit for the result. Paul says neither the one who plants that seed nor the one who follows with "water" (i.e., teaching and encouragement, etc.) produces that new faith. Both are merely workers in God's field. We are God's hired help obeying the call to go, but the credit for the result belongs to God alone, who produces new life in the believer by His Spirit and makes the growth possible. God receives all the credit for creating and building the Church. As Paul says:

> But by His doing you are in Christ Jesus, who became to us wisdom from God, and righteousness and sanctification, and redemption, so that, just as it is written, "LET HIM WHO BOASTS, BOAST IN THE LORD."
> —*1 Cor. 1:30-31*

So, if God causes all the growth of new faith, what part do we play in bringing people to faith? Here's where a transactional, *quid pro quo* mindset can really impede a Christian's spiritual growth. If we think God responds to us, then we naturally misunderstand how people are saved and why God calls us to participate in evangelism. We come to view the process of being saved as a transaction itself.

In the Great Commission, the Lord asks us to take three steps of action. Apart from the initial step of evangelism (which we'll discuss later), our first response to a newly converted believer is to baptize them. Baptism serves several purposes, but in this context, it's an essential test of sincerity. When someone claims to have accepted the gospel, they admit their sinfulness and confess their faith in Jesus as their Messiah — the only way they can be reconciled to the Father. But we must question their sincerity if they can't bring themselves to be immersed in water to publicly express their commitment in front of likeminded witnesses. Notice that in the Great Commission, Jesus didn't say the *Church* baptizes. This isn't a responsibility reserved for just the pastor or the staff. This is the responsibility of every believer and, as we'll explore later, can be as simple as an impromptu immersion on a desert road.

Second, we are to teach new believers to obey all that Jesus commanded His disciples. This is where we get our notion of discipleship: receiving new believers and nourishing them with the fundamental principles of living according to the faith they received through Christ. We can disciple through small group studies, individual mentorships, or simply sharing our personal walk: believers edifying other believers to mature and grow strong in the Body of Christ.

Thus, Jesus' Great Commission includes the instruction for us to make disciples of the nations by baptizing new believers and teaching them to grow in the grace and knowledge of Jesus Christ. Before we can do those things, we must first reach the unbeliever, as the Great Commission commands. Some might say the Great Commission includes converting unbelievers to believers, but that's only partially true.

God works through people to bring the Good News to others. In Greek, the word "evangelist" means "one who brings good tidings." Through His appointed evangelists (workers in the field like Paul and Apollos), God brings new life and new growth to a lost and dying world. In that sense, the Great Commission involves faithful men and women in bringing the gospel to unbelievers so they may be converted. But it's notable that in His Great Commission, Jesus made no reference to our responsibility for producing new faith. Rather, Jesus placed the emphasis squarely on receiving that new spiritual life, confirming it, and helping it mature through discipleship.

In this way, our commission is like the role of a doctor assisting in the birth of a child. The doctor isn't responsible for forming the child in the mother's womb, shaping the structures of the body, or making the heart beat. God does those things. The doctor simply stands at the end of the assembly line and receives the new life as it is born. Then he washes it and hands the new life over to caretakers. who begin to instruct it and bring it up in the ways of the Lord. This is the essence of the Great Commission — and He's asking all of us to take part.

> *He said to them, "But who do you say that I am?"*
>
> *Simon Peter answered, "You are the Christ, the Son of the living God."*
>
> *And Jesus said to him, "Blessed are you, Simon Barjona, because flesh and blood did not reveal this to you, but My Father who is in Heaven."*
> **—Matt. 16:15–17**

Flesh and blood didn't teach Peter that Jesus was the Messiah. Only God can reveal that truth through His Holy Spirit. Evangelism without the Holy Spirit is just words. We would do well to remember that the birth of new life, whether physical or spiritual, is the work of God through His Holy Spirit. What does an evangelist bring to the process? Paul answered that question in one short verse:

> *So faith comes from hearing, and hearing by the Word of Christ.*
> **—Rom. 10:17**

When the evangelist does his work by preaching God's Word, the Holy Spirit opens the unbeliever's heart to faith. According to Ephesians 6:17, God's Word is the sword of the Spirit, and Hebrews 4:12 tells us the Word pierces the heart. It is the instrument by which the Holy Spirit brings faith, and the world needs believing men and women to deliver the Word to lost and unbelieving people. God's Word may reach an unbeliever from the pages of the Bible, or it may come from the mouth of an evangelist — but in either case, the Word of Christ is the tool the Holy Spirit uses to produce faith.

> *Therefore, I make known to you that no one speaking by the Spirit of God says, "Jesus is accursed"; and no one can say, "Jesus is Lord," except by the Holy Spirit.*
> **—1 Cor. 12:3**

Clearly, God is sovereign in evangelism and the birth of new life, but He invites us to participate in His work. However, if we're not careful, we may begin to claim some measure of credit for any success we experience. Sadly, many churches seem to have lost sight of the sovereignty of God in evangelism. Many churches have produced entire generations of Christians who believe everything depends on them personally. Some have even been taught that if they do not share the gospel message, they have somehow participated in sealing another person's fate in eternity — that they share responsibility for the person's condemnation. However, just as no one deserves credit for another person's salvation, no one can be guilty of another person's sin and condemnation. Moreover, God is not dependent on our obedience to bring the Good News to another. Remember Saul on the road to Damascus, intending to persecute Christians. God revealed truth to him without the aid of another person. And yet, God found a man, Ananias, who would be obedient to disciple Saul into Paul.

Does God's sovereignty in salvation give us license to ignore the Great Commission? May it never be! Each of us face personal consequences when we neglect our responsibility to obey that commission. Remember the earlier passage from 1 Corinthians, where Paul mentions rewards for the workers in God's field:

> *Now the one who plants and the one who waters are one; but each will receive their own reward according to their own labor.*
> *—1 Cor. 3:8*

If we are lazy workers who don't do our part in the field, God will simply hire other workers to get the job done. It's His field, and He will not let His crop suffer due to the mistakes of poor workers. Then, the obedient workers will receive the wages (heavenly rewards) that could have been ours.

There is another mistake we can make as workers in God's fields — one that is not often taught. It's different from being lazy, and it can have even more dire consequences for the Church. It comes when we lose sight of the real meaning of the Great Commission and shift our focus to making believers, rather than discipling new believers. Consider the example of Simon in the book of Acts.

Acts chapter 8 begins with Saul approving the death of an early evangelist, Stephen. After Stephen was stoned to death for his testimony, wide-scale persecution broke out in Jerusalem. This persecution resulted in scattering many of the young Church's leaders to areas outside Jerusalem, and the Word was preached beyond the city — persecution turned into growth. One of the leaders who left Jerusalem was Philip, who traveled to Samaria. Jews rarely traveled there, since Samaritans and Jews generally despised one another.

> *Philip went down to the city of Samaria and began proclaiming Christ to them. The crowds with one accord were giving attention to what was said by Philip, as they heard and saw the signs which he was performing. For in the case of many who had unclean spirits, they were coming out of them shouting with a loud voice; and many who had been paralyzed and lame were healed. So there was much rejoicing in that city.*
>
> *Now there was a man named Simon, who formerly was practicing magic in the city and astonishing the people of Samaria, claiming to be someone great; and they all, from smallest to greatest, were giving attention to him, saying, "This man is what is called the Great Power of God." And they were giving him attention because he had for a long time astonished them with his magic arts. But when they believed Philip preaching the good news about the kingdom of God and the name of Jesus Christ, they were being*

baptized, men and women alike. Even Simon himself believed; and after being baptized, he continued on with Philip, and as he observed signs and great miracles taking place, he was constantly amazed.
—*Acts 8:5-13*

The Gospel of Mark tells us that before Christ left the disciples, He told them they would have unique spiritual powers to aid in spreading the gospel message. Among those powers were the ability to cast out demons and the laying on of hands to heal the sick. Here, we see Philip doing just that.

Another interesting aspect of Philip's story is this man named Simon, who had been practicing magic in Samaria for some time. The story makes clear that he had real power, but his was demonic power: the black arts. He used this power to astonish the Samaritans, and he gained considerable attention and respect from them. The people there even claimed he had the Great Power of God, which sounds suspiciously like a counterfeit version of the Holy Spirit. Then Philip arrived, and with him, the true Power of God.

Philip began to use the authority of Jesus' name to perform the miracles Jesus said he would, and he amazed the city. This city was already accustomed to amazing spectacles, yet many people believed and were baptized after Philip began his work. Simon was amazed as well, and Scripture says that he, too, believed and was baptized. Simon then continued on with Philip, intent on observing the miracles Philip was performing.

Thus far, this is an encouraging story of Philip's gift in evangelism, but the story continues:

> *Now when the apostles in Jerusalem heard that Samaria had received the Word of God, they sent them Peter and John, who came down and prayed for them that they might receive the Holy Spirit. For the Spirit had not yet fallen upon any of them; they had simply been baptized in the name of the Lord Jesus. Then they began laying their hands on them, and they were receiving the Holy Spirit.*
>
> *Now when Simon saw that the Spirit was bestowed through the laying on of the apostles' hands, he offered them money, saying, "Give this authority to me as well, so that everyone on whom I lay my hands may receive the Holy Spirit."*
>
> *But Peter said to him, "May your silver perish with you, because you thought you could obtain the gift of God with money! You have no part or portion in this matter, for your heart is not right before God. Therefore, repent of this wickedness of yours, and pray to the Lord that, if possible, the intention of your heart may be forgiven you. For I see that you are in the gall of bitterness and in the bondage of iniquity."*
>
> *But Simon answered and said, "Pray to the Lord for me yourselves, so that nothing of what you have said may come upon me."*
> —*Acts 8:14–24*

While the persecution in Jerusalem scattered many within the Church like Philip, the Apostles steadfastly remained in the city. However, as they began to receive word that Gentiles — and even Samaritans — were responding to the gospel, they were eager to confirm the rumors for themselves. Scripture says something puzzling here: the believers in Samaria did not receive the Holy Spirit when they confessed and were baptized. The gift of the indwelling Holy Spirit for every believer is a unique characteristic of the Church since Pentecost. The early

Church believers were sealed with the Holy Spirit by the laying on of hands as an undeniable sign of Jesus's promise. The Father later ceased giving such immediately visible signs of the Holy Spirit's arrival because He wants our faith to lead us, not our sight. We believe in faith the things that are unseen. According to Scripture, the Holy Spirit now indwells us the moment we believe (Acts 2:38, Ephesians 1:13), but back in Samaria, the new believers waited for the Apostles to lay hands on them to receive the Holy Spirit. The text makes it clear that bestowing the Holy Spirit was a visible and impressive procedure — impressive enough for Simon to want a piece of the action.

Simon declared himself Philip's disciple and followed him constantly, trying to learn the secrets of his impressive powers. Finally, after Simon watched the Apostles bestowing the Holy Spirit by laying on hands, he couldn't endure any longer and offered money for their powers. Now, earlier we read that Simon believed and was baptized, so you may be uncomfortable with this characterization of Simon as someone who faked his confession of faith. Fake confessions do occur. That's why Peter and John made strong points in their letters that we should be discerning. Looking again at our story, we see the Apostles themselves talked with Simon to discern his motives, causing Peter to say, "May your silver perish with you." In Greek, Peter said, "Go to hell with your money." — and he meant it literally. Then he said, "You have no part or portion in this matter." A look at this statement in Greek reveals:

Part = *meris* = no share

Portion = *kleros* = inheritance

Matter = *logos* = word (As used in John 1:1: "In the beginning was the Word, and the Word was with God, and the Word was God.")

In other words, Peter said, "You have no share, no inheritance in the Word." He then told Simon that his heart was not right before God and he needed to repent and pray for forgiveness. But here Peter made a stunning qualifier: "Pray to the Lord that, *if possible*, the intention of your heart may be forgiven you." For a believer, there is never any doubt concerning God's forgiveness. Had Simon been a believer, he would already have been forgiven for that sin and every other sin he could possibly commit. Yet in this case, Peter indicated there was doubt as to whether God would forgive his sin. Moreover, Peter said that Simon was "in the gall of bitterness and bondage of iniquity." Interestingly, Peter began that statement with the word *horao*, which means "perceive." Peter perceived something about Simon that couldn't necessarily be seen. "Gall of bitterness" is a colloquial phrase common in Scripture, and it always means the intense envy of another person, bordering on hatred. Simon envied these powerful men so much, he was consumed by it. Furthermore, Simon was in the bondage of iniquity, a slave to sin rather than a slave to Christ. Peter discerned that Simon was an unbeliever, and Simon responded by asking Peter to pray for him. This is the classic response of unbelievers. Since they have no relationship with God, they seek someone else to pray for them.

This story in Acts is an example of the second, more insidious risk in evangelism. When we lose sight of the Great Commission's real meaning, shifting our focus to making believers rather than discipling new believers, we risk filling our churches with Simons. In the early Church, the Apostles came and delivered the Word, then discerned the result through discipleship. Today, few churches make discipleship the emphasis of their evangelism effort. In fact, most churches have separated their evangelism and discipleship ministries, but baptism and discipleship prove the effectiveness of our evangelism efforts, revealing the Simons. Too many churches have become content to fill seats with people, rather than filling hearts with the Word of God. For example, what percentage of new believers are being baptized today? How many are then taken aside and personally discipled to grow in the knowledge and grace of Jesus Christ by regular participation in solid Bible study programs? Not many, according to the observations of the researcher George Barna:

Our studies consistently show that churches base their sense of success on indicators such as attendance, congregant satisfaction, dollars raised and built-out square footage. None of those factors relates to the kind of radical shift in thinking and behavior that Jesus Christ died on the cross to facilitate. As long as we measure success on the basis of popularity and efficiency, we will continue to see a nation filled with people who can recite Bible stories but fail to live according to Bible principles.[10]

One reason for this is that the Church has jettisoned its solemn responsibility to confirm new faith and disciple it. Churches have replaced discipleship with superficial weekly experiences that merely fill a square on our calendars. While a given congregation may not be part of the problem, as parts of the whole Body of Christ, we all share the blame. Thankfully, the rest of Acts chapter 8 shows us how evangelism can work hand in hand with discipleship. After Philip left Samaria, he heard from the Holy Spirit, which led him to a new experience:

> *But an angel of the Lord spoke to Philip saying, "Get up and go south to the road that descends from Jerusalem to Gaza." (This is a desert road.)*
>
> *So he got up and went; and there was an Ethiopian eunuch, a court official of Candace, queen of the Ethiopians, who was in charge of all her treasure; and he had come to Jerusalem to worship, and he was returning and sitting in his chariot, and was reading the prophet Isaiah.*
>
> *Then the Spirit said to Philip, "Go up and join this chariot."*
>
> *Philip ran up and heard him reading Isaiah the prophet, and said, "Do you understand what you are reading?"*
>
> *And he said, "Well, how could I, unless someone guides me?" And he invited Philip to come up and sit with him.*
>
> *Now the passage of Scripture which he was reading was this: "HE WAS LED AS A SHEEP TO SLAUGHTER; AND AS A LAMB BEFORE ITS SHEARER IS SILENT, SO HE DOES NOT OPEN HIS MOUTH. IN HUMILIATION HIS JUDGMENT WAS TAKEN AWAY; WHO WILL RELATE HIS GENERATION? FOR HIS LIFE IS REMOVED FROM THE EARTH."*
>
> *The eunuch answered Philip and said, "Please tell me, of whom does the prophet say this? Of himself or of someone else?"*

> Then Philip opened his mouth and beginning from this Scripture he preached Jesus to him.
>
> As they went along the road they came to some water; and the eunuch said, "Look! Water! What prevents me from being baptized?"
>
> And Philip said, "If you believe with all your heart, you may." And he answered and said, "I believe that Jesus Christ is the Son of God."
>
> And he ordered the chariot to stop; and they both went down into the water, Philip as well as the eunuch, and he baptized him.
>
> When they came up out of the water, the Spirit of the Lord snatched Philip away; and the eunuch no longer saw him but went on his way rejoicing.
> —*Acts 8:26–39*

It's significant that this appears in the same chapter as the account of Simon, because it stands in stark contrast to the events in Samaria. Where one experience depends on miraculous signs and wonders, the other relies on the Word of God. One experience waits for the Holy Spirit to confirm faith; the other has the Holy Spirit involved even before it begins. The Spirit calls Philip to go out into the field. Philip responds, like a worker entering his field — for the fields are white for the harvest. The Spirit prepares the ground, representing the heart of a person, to receive the seed of the Word of God. The Spirit directs Philip to that person, where the sowing begins. As the eunuch endeavors to understand the Word, he falls short and needs someone to explain its meaning. The Holy Spirit prompts Philip to join the man and explain the truth, and faith begins to grow. New faith prompts obedience, so the man seeks baptism and Philip complies. Here is our worker completing his assigned task, as the Master moves him to new ground, leaving others to nurture the rejoicing new believer. What a beautiful scene, and what a simple picture of how God does the work yet invites us to join Him.

When we are ready to obey the Great Commission, we should model our ministry after the second half of Acts 8. Key to that will be listening to the Holy Spirit, watching for signs that He has prepared the heart of an unbeliever and given them ears to hear the gospel through the Word of God. Our emphasis should be on baptism, as a confirmation of new faith, and discipling the new believer in the meat of the Word through the love of the Church. However, we should remember Jesus' words when He told us not to throw our pearls before swine (Matthew 7:6). There is a time when an unbeliever is prepared to receive the gospel and a time when he or she won't. We should not give up prematurely, but rather wait to see the Holy Spirit tilling the ground. Otherwise, we will be wasting our efforts in the wrong "field" of an unreceptive heart. We should look instead for those who are waiting and ready to invite you into their chariot. That's the work of evangelism to which God has invited us.

The work of evangelism is to bring the gospel to those whose hearts have been prepared by the Holy Spirit to receive Christ as their Savior and be born into eternal life. During His earthly ministry, Jesus was directly confronted with the question, "What shall I do to obtain eternal life?" on two recorded occasions. This is a bold question, and considering the gravity of Jesus' teachings, it's surprising it is so seldom recorded in Scripture. In these instances,

Jesus demonstrated His instruction not to cast pearls before swine and not to present the gospel message to hearts not prepared by the Holy Spirit.

Luke chapter 10 records the question for the first time, as the seventy disciples return from their mission of preparing every city and place Christ Himself will visit. These seventy disciples overflow with joy at their works in the Name of the Lord. Jesus speaks a spontaneous prayer that conveys a strong message of God's sovereignty in salvation:

> *At that very time He rejoiced greatly in the Holy Spirit, and said, "I praise You, O Father, Lord of Heaven and earth, that You have hidden these things from the wise and intelligent and have revealed them to infants. Yes, Father, for this way was well-pleasing in Your sight."*
>
> *"All things have been handed over to Me by My Father, and no one knows who the Son is except the Father, and who the Father is except the Son, and anyone to whom the Son wills to reveal Him."*
>
> *Turning to the disciples, He said privately, "Blessed are the eyes which see the things you see, for I say to you, that many prophets and kings wished to see the things which you see, and did not see them, and to hear the things which you hear, and did not hear them."*
> —*Luke 10:21-24*

Jesus praises the Father for revealing the gospel message to the humblest of the world, rather than to those who profess to be wise — the Pharisees, the spiritual leaders of Jesus's day, who claimed to know God and how to please Him. They were anything but pleasing to God, leading others astray with their false doctrines. In contrast, God was content to reveal the truth to those who weren't looking for Him and who never saw themselves as righteous, but as sinners. Further, Jesus adds that the knowledge of the gospel is something reserved for those to whom the Son wills to reveal it. This is a profound statement that should cause rejoicing in those to whom God has revealed His Son.

At the heart of the gospel is the distinction between the self-righteous and the humble, and Jesus uses it to remind the disciples how special their situation truly is. Throughout Israel's history, generations of holy people had understood the Messianic prophecies and longed to see the day of His coming, but they weren't granted that privilege. They longed, Jesus said, to experience what the disciples saw and heard. Instead, these ordinary people ("infants") received that honor. He chose the humble over the wise to receive the Messiah of the world at this time.

Immediately following Jesus' prayer, a lawyer in the crowd stands up and asks that bold question, "What shall I do to inherit eternal life?"

> *And a lawyer stood up and put Him to the test, saying, "Teacher, what shall I do to inherit eternal life?"*
>
> *And He said to him, "What is written in the Law? How does it read to you?"*
>
> *And he answered, "YOU SHALL LOVE THE LORD YOUR GOD WITH ALL YOUR HEAR, AND WITH ALL YOUR SOUL, AND WITH ALL YOUR STRENGTH, AND WITH ALL YOUR MIND; AND YOUR NEIGHBOR AS YOURSELF."*

And He said to him, "You have answered correctly; DO THIS AND YOU WILL LIVE."
—**Luke 10:25-28**

This encounter opens with a legitimate question, one that every believer has asked at some point, but like Simon the Magician, this man is not a believer. His motive is not to seek the truth about how to receive eternal life, but to discredit Jesus by drawing Him into a debate about the Law. Answering the challenge, Jesus turns to the Law, effectively asking the lawyer to answer his own question — and the man answers correctly! Normally, this would be a great victory for the lawyer. He has engaged a popular rabbi with a question of infinite importance. Also, by citing a couple of commandments in just a few sentences, he wins the rabbi's concession that he has the right answer. Not only is it the right answer, but it is also the one that brings eternal life!

However, this is no victory. It is a bitter defeat, because the lawyer turns to the Law, the ministry of death, as Paul calls it, to find the answer to eternal life. In Matthew 22, Jesus says that the two commandments the lawyer cited are the commandments upon which the whole Law depends. Thus, the lawyer's answer could be read, "Fulfill the Law perfectly and you will live." However, the purpose of the Law was to prove to people that it was impossible to achieve that standard. Its purpose was to turn people to Christ's righteousness. Christ has not chosen to reveal Himself to this lawyer, so he is incapable of understanding the Source of true righteousness. He has zeal for the Law but no real knowledge of its truth. Paul describes this situation by speaking of the Jews who would not receive Christ:

> *For I testify about them that they have a zeal for God, but not in accordance with knowledge. For not knowing about God's righteousness and seeking to establish their own, they did not subject themselves to the righteousness of God.*
> —*Rom. 10:2-3*

Those who do not know God's righteousness create their own path to salvation. And that's exactly what this lawyer does when he recognizes it is impossible to achieve righteousness under the Law:

> *But wishing to justify himself, he said to Jesus, "And who is my neighbor?"*
>
> *Jesus replied and said, "A man was going down from Jerusalem to Jericho, and fell among robbers, and they stripped him and beat him, and went away leaving him half dead. And by chance a priest was going down on that road, and when he saw him, he passed by on the other side.*
>
> *Likewise, a Levite also, when he came to the place and saw him, passed by on the other side. But a Samaritan, who was on a journey, came upon him; and when he saw him, he felt compassion, and came to him and bandaged up his wounds, pouring oil and wine on them; and he put him on his own beast, and brought him to an inn and took care of him. On the next day he took out two denarii and gave them to the innkeeper and said, 'Take care of him; and whatever more you spend, when I return, I will repay you.'"*
>
> *"Which of these three do you think proved to be a neighbor to the man who fell into the robbers' hands?"*

And he said, "The one who showed mercy toward him."

Then Jesus said to him, "Go and do the same."
—**Luke 10:29–37**

By seeking to justify himself by his own righteousness, the lawyer employs a common practice of his time. When confronted with the impossibility of keeping the Law, he turns to the letter of the Law and away from its spirit — but the letter kills. He has doubled down on a literal dead-end, but Christ confronts him on this by comparing the attitude of a Levite, a seemingly righteous man, with the attitude of a lowly Samaritan. The Levite undoubtedly knew the letter of the Law but failed to live out its spirit. The Samaritan would never have been regarded as wise in the Law, nor righteous in it, but he did live out its spirit. This would be anathema to the lawyer. Jesus tells him not to model himself after the priest or the Levite, but after the Samaritan who acted selflessly toward a man who probably held him in contempt. In his current state, it's impossible for this lawyer to go and do the same. He is left with the book answer to how he can obtain eternal life, but not the practical answer of how to *receive* it.

The second time Jesus is confronted with the question about how to obtain eternal life, it comes from a man known as the rich young ruler. All three synoptic Gospels record the story:

And someone came to Him and said, "Teacher, what good thing shall I do that I may obtain eternal life?"

And He said to him, "Why are you asking Me about what is

> *good? There is only One who is good; but if you wish to enter into life, keep the commandments."*
>
> *Then he said to Him, "Which ones?"*
>
> *And Jesus said, "YOU SHALL NOT COMMIT MURDER; YOU SHALL NOT COMMIT ADULTERY; YOU SHALL NOT STEAL; YOU SHALL NOT BEAR FALSE WITNESS; HONOR YOUR FATHER AND MOTHER; and YOU SHALL LOVE YOUR NEIGHBOR AS YOURSELF."*
>
> *The young man said to Him, "All these things I have kept; what am I still lacking?"*
>
> *Jesus said to him, "If you wish to be complete, go and sell your possessions and give to the poor, and you will have treasure in Heaven; and come, follow Me."*
>
> *But when the young man heard this statement, he went away grieving; for he was one who owned much property.*
> —Matt. 19:16-22

Unlike the lawyer, the rich young ruler seems sincere in his motives. This man wants to be a part of the Kingdom; but Christ, knowing the man's heart, answers with a peculiar question: "Why are you asking Me about what is good? There is only One who is good." Jesus knows this man has placed his trust in his earthly works and accomplishments — earthly works that are unrighteous by definition and can therefore be measured only by comparison. This man measures his own earthly riches by comparing them to the riches of others. He considers his abundance evidence of his righteousness before God. In response, Jesus points the man to the absolute standard of righteousness, the Father.

Since the man is still focused on what he can *do*, Jesus directs him to the Law and tells him to keep the commandments. At this point, the man asks his own peculiar question: "Which ones?" Scripture is clear on the answer: all of them – righteousness must be absolute. His question reveals that he knows he can't keep the Law perfectly, so he looks for a sliding scale, and momentarily, Jesus gives him one: you shall love your neighbor as yourself.

Christ places His focus on the earthward commandments, those governing human interactions. Given the man's self-confidence that he has fulfilled those commandments, we might wonder why he doesn't simply say, "Thank you, Teacher," and walk away. Perhaps because he feels convicted of a need to justify himself, he presses on to learn what he still lacks. Jesus' answer sharply moves the discussion from the earthly to the heavenly. By telling the man to sell all he has and follow Him, Jesus challenges the man to move his trust from the carnal to God — in short, to have faith in God. The man's trust in the visible is evidence of his lack of faith in the unseen. After all, if the man truly believes he will eventually be part of an eternal Kingdom, he would be willing to trade his treasure in this world for the one to come.

> *And without faith it is impossible to please Him, for the one who comes to God must believe that He is and that He is a rewarder of those who seek Him.*
> —***Heb. 11:6***

The rich young ruler's response shows he lacks faith in a heavenly reward. Compare this to the saving faith of Peter, who was clearly expecting a reward:

> *Then Peter said to Him, "Behold, we have left everything and followed You; what then will there be for us?"*
>
> *And Jesus said to them, "Truly I say to you, that you who have followed Me, at the renewal of all things when the Son of Man will sit on His glorious throne, you also shall sit upon twelve thrones, judging the twelve tribes of Israel."*
> **—Matt. 19:27-28**

The rich young ruler lacks faith in this heavenly reward, trusting in earthly riches rather than in the Kingdom. He embraces his earthly wealth as a sign of God's approval, and the disciples seem to share his confusion. Astonished when they hear it is difficult for a rich man to enter the kingdom of heaven, they ask Jesus, "Then who can be saved?"

Jesus was directly confronted with the question of what someone must *do* to obtain eternal life. In both cases, we learned it is impossible to obtain eternal life by *doing*. However, in another encounter, Jesus revealed the path to entering the kingdom of heaven to a man who didn't even have the chance to ask.

> *Now there was a man of the Pharisees, named Nicodemus, a ruler of the Jews; this man came to Jesus by night and said to Him, "Rabbi, we know that You have come from God as a teacher; for no one can do these signs that You do unless God is with him."*

> *Jesus answered and said to him, "Truly, truly, I say to you, unless one is born again, he cannot see the kingdom of God."*
>
> *Nicodemus said to Him, "How can a man be born when he is old? He cannot enter a second time into his mother's womb and be born, can he?"*
>
> *Jesus answered, "Truly, truly, I say to you, unless one is born of water and the Spirit he cannot enter into the kingdom of God. That which is born of the flesh is flesh, and that which is born of the Spirit is spirit".*
>
> *Jesus answered and said to him, "Are you the teacher of Israel and do not understand these things?"*
> —*John 3:1-10*

Nicodemus opened the conversation with a respectful concession that Jesus was from God. Jesus saw his heart and moved directly to the question on his mind: how to enter the Kingdom of God (obtain eternal life). Jesus gave Nicodemus a different explanation compared to the ones He provided in the previous encounters we've examined. Jesus made no reference to the Law in responding to Nicodemus. Instead, He answered using a very interesting metaphor: being born again.

The choice of birth as a metaphor is telling because the phrase "birth in Christ" teaches us about the manner of our salvation. Being born again spiritually is like being born physically. Consider that for a moment. Our physical birth happens *to* us because of a decision made by our parents. We don't choose to be born, or when we are born; we're oblivious, and it just happens. In response to Nicodemus's amazement, Jesus elaborated:

> *"Do not be amazed that I said to you, 'You must be born again.' The wind blows where it wishes and you hear the sound of it, but do not know where it comes from and where it is going; so is everyone who is born of the Spirit." Nicodemus said to Him, "How can these things be?"*
> —*John 3:7–9*

Jesus described God's sovereignty in salvation. The Holy Spirit goes where the Father chooses to send Him, preparing the hearts of people to accept the gospel and be born again into eternal life as new creations. This happens according to God's will. Being born again can't happen by our own will, because we were born into this world spiritually dead. We could not comprehend spiritual things. Without the power of the Holy Spirit, we would never have understood we were spiritually dead and needed to be born again.

> *But a natural person does not accept the things of the Spirit of God, for they are foolishness to them; and they cannot understand them, because they are spiritually appraised.*
> —*1 Cor. 2:14*

How can we gain the power of the Spirit to understand spiritual truth and accept Christ? Consider the story of Lazarus in John's Gospel. The Lord intentionally allowed Lazarus to die and decay in the tomb for three days. When Jesus arrived to resurrect Lazarus and prove His power over death, He didn't ask Lazarus if he wanted to be restored to life. If He had, Lazarus could not have responded — he was dead. Dead things know nothing and cannot hear or agree to anything. First, Jesus made him live, and only then could Lazarus respond to Christ's order to come out of the darkness of the tomb into the light of the day. Jesus' words were life. So it is for us spiritually. Just as Jesus raised Lazarus, and the Father raised Christ, so we too need to be raised spiritually, so that we can come to faith.

> But God, being rich in mercy, because of His great love with which He loved us, even when we were dead in our transgressions, made us alive together with Christ (by grace you have been saved), and raised us up with Him, and seated us with Him in the Heavenly places in Christ Jesus, so that in the ages to come He might show the surpassing riches of His grace in kindness toward us in Christ Jesus.
> —*Eph. 2:4–7*

This is the very definition of *grace*. Grace is the undeserved favor of God toward those who are dead and do not know they need to be restored to life. Grace begins the work of restoration for those who are not even aware it has begun.

> For by grace you have been saved through faith; and that not of yourselves, it is the gift of God; not as a result of works, so that no one may boast. For we are His workmanship, created in Christ Jesus for good works, which God prepared beforehand so that we would walk in them.
> —*Eph. 2:8–10*

The concept of unmerited favor leads us to a vital truth about God's sovereignty in our salvation. God chose His children — those who would enter salvation through Jesus Christ.

> *...just as He chose us in Him before the foundation of the world, that we would be holy and blameless before Him. In love He predestined us to adoption as sons and daughters through Jesus Christ to Himself, according to the kind intention of His will...*
> —**Eph. 1:4-5**

Before God formed the world, He already had His children in mind and had selected them for salvation. Though they hadn't been physically born yet, millions of believers were already under the New Covenant when Christ died on the cross. God's plan unfolded, and in time, they were born, and then born again. The Father's timing is all-important. If God chose us at some point during our lifetime, we might conclude it was due to something we did. Remember the earlier question, "What good thing must *I do* to inherit eternal life?" The Lord doesn't want us to misunderstand how we found ourselves in Christ. It wasn't by virtue of a family line or some good thing we did. We didn't earn it, nor did we know it was coming.

The fact that the Father chose us should be of great comfort. If God planned to bless us before the Creation itself, we can be assured we will receive those spiritual blessings. What *inside* Creation can challenge a decision God made *before* Creation? As Jesus described in His Parable of the Lost Sheep (Matthew 18:12–14; Luke 15:3–7), the number of God's sheep is specific, and He will be seeking them actively until the fold is full. God will never be content if even one is lost. He will leave the 99 to find just one.

We've looked at three interactions where Christ dealt with the question of how to find eternal life. It is worth noting that in Scripture, references to humility precede each instance. In one, Christ rejoices that the Father is revealed to infants. In the other, He contrasts the publican and the Pharisee. These examples remind us that Christ elevates the humble and humbles the self-righteous. The lawyer and the rich young ruler were among those who appeared to be wise. Therein lies a great irony: he only two men recorded in the Gospels who directly asked Christ how they might obtain eternal life didn't understand they were spiritually dead.

By attempting to test Jesus on this question, the lawyer clearly thought he already had the answer, and in fact, he did. The problem was that until he was exposed to the Light, he didn't understand it is impossible to obtain eternal life by *doing*. Following His encounter with the rich young ruler, Christ Himself declared that impossibility. Though the ruler seemed to seek eternal life, he didn't really believe he was spiritually dead, or he would have been happy to sell all he had to obtain the life he supposedly sought. We are all born into this world spiritually dead and are therefore susceptible to the original satanic lie spoken in the Garden, which has evolved from "you surely will not die" to "surely you aren't dead." The dead can't hear anything. Both the lawyer and the rich young ruler knew the Scriptures, but neither could understand them.

The conversation with Nicodemus was entirely different. Nicodemus humbled himself and acknowledged that Christ was sent from God. As a ruler of the Jews and teacher of Israel, Nicodemus would certainly appear wise to others. The difference here was that he no longer appeared wise to himself. Seeing his humility, Christ spoke directly to what was on Nicodemus's heart. There was no discussion of the Law; instead, Christ revealed the mystery of the Holy Spirit and His work in preparing people to receive spiritual birth. And there is evidence, both in his later defense of Jesus and participation in His burial, that Nicodemus did receive that spiritual birth (John 3:1–21).

It does not please God to glorify those who think they have earned salvation by their own power. The question is not, "How do *I obtain* eternal life," but rather, "How does *God give* eternal life?" Many people have their own ideas about how to please God to serve their own interests. But it is by His grace, through faith alone, that we enter His glory and become His child — a decision He made in His sovereignty from the foundations of the world.

CHAPTER SIX

God vs. Satan

On April 20, 1999, two teenagers entered their high school in Littleton, Colorado, and systematically murdered 19 people before taking their own lives. On September 11, 2001, terrorists highjacked four airliners, flying them into the World Trade Center, the Pentagon, and a field in Pennsylvania, resulting in the deaths of 3,076 people. On December 26, 2004, an earthquake in the Indian Ocean produced a tsunami that destroyed coastlines from East Africa to Indonesia, resulting in the deaths of more than 174,000 people. These three dramatic events, separated by time and great distances, appear to have little in common. Each took their death toll from different communities, with different causes and consequences. But for all their differences, each shared at least one thing in common: All three events so shocked the conscience and stunned the world by their horror and senselessness that they prompted a common question: how could a loving God permit such things to happen?

Of the seven topics this book covers regarding the sovereignty of God, none will make so obvious, and yet so controversial, an opening statement as this: God is sovereign over every event that occurs in all His Creation throughout all time. This truth is self-evident, because there can be no higher power in all Creation than the Creator Himself. The God who has the power to, at His Word, speak into existence the entire universe and all that fills it, must by necessity have all power and authority over it. There is no other power that could possibly contend with, much less match, the power of God. Whether by His active intervention, or by His willful restraint, God purposes all things to occur exactly as they do. In fact, when we ask the question, "How can God *allow* such things?" we are indirectly acknowledging that God has the capability to prevent such things. This prompts us to ask, "Why didn't He prevent them?" Charles Spurgeon addressed this question:[11]

> *I believe that every particle of dust that dances in the sunbeam does not move an atom more or less than God wishes — that every particle of spray that dashes against the steamboat has its orbit, as well as the sun in the Heavens — that the chaff from the hand of the winnower is steered as the stars in their courses. The creeping of an aphid over the rosebud is as much fixed as the march of the devastating pestilence — the fall of ... leaves from a poplar is as fully ordained as the tumbling of an avalanche.*
> —***Spurgeon, 1857***

It can be unsettling to consider all that Scripture has to say about God's control over the events of history. We find ourselves wrestling with issues of evil, sin, and humanity's relationship to God. We often begin our exploration by first drawing a line in the sand, declaring that God's sovereignty goes only so far and we control the rest. Then, we read details in Scripture that force us to erase our first line and redraw it a little closer to us and a little farther from God.

The issue of God's sovereignty is not some abstract, unprofitable debate reserved for pastors and theologians. Understanding the extent of God's authority and ability to control world events cuts to the core of our faith and its meaning. It is the foundation for our confidence in Old Testament prophecies and our hope in New Testament promises. His ability to exercise control over all space, time, and matter is the very definition of what it means for Him to be the true Living God we desire to worship. This discussion is important, for if we can cast doubt on God's sovereignty over all He created and all He declared by His Word, then we will also cast doubt on His ability to fulfill His promises to us. And if there is doubt God can fulfill His promises according to His will, then as Paul said in his first letter to the Corinthians, we of all people are most to be pitied (1 Corinthians 15:19).

Opinions on the issue of God's sovereignty over His Creation generally fall into one of three groups, at least among those who believe in a higher power:

1. God created the world and the universe, and then, like someone spinning a top, He stood back to watch it work itself to conclusion. Now,

God's hand never touches His Creation or intervenes in its course.

2. God created the world and occasionally intervenes, naturally and supernaturally, to change the course of history, always for good purpose — accomplishing the outcome He desires through those events. Implicit in this view is the principle that some things lie outside God's sovereign control. Evil, for example, would be an independent force operating apart from God's desires and will. This view also holds that humans themselves operate free from the direct control of God, and God would not intervene to change the will of humans.

3. God created the world and now sustains and controls everything in it. He doesn't just intervene to occasionally redirect history; He writes literally every page of history. Daniel 2:21 says He changes the times and the seasons and puts rulers in their place so that everything will happen according to a preordained plan.

The third group holds the view that there are no limits to God's sovereignty. The 1689 Confession of Faith for the historic Reformed Baptist movement in London gives us one such example:

God who, in infinite power and wisdom, has created all things, upholds, directs, controls, and governs them, both animate and inanimate, great and small, by a providence supremely wise and holy, and in accordance with His infallible foreknowledge and the free and immutable decisions of His will. He fulfills the purposes for which He created them, so that His wisdom, power, and justice, together with His infinite goodness and mercy, might be praised and glorified. Nothing happens by chance or outside the sphere of God's providence. As God is the First Cause of all events, they happen immutable and infallibly according to His foreknowledge and decree, to which they stand related. Yet by His providence God controls them, that second causes, operating either as fixed laws, or freely, or in dependence upon other causes, play their part in bringing them about.

Critics of this view describe it as fatalism, to which Charles Spurgeon, a member of this third group, replied:

What is fate? Fate is this — Whatever is, must be. But there is a difference between that and Providence. Providence says, Whatever God ordains, must be; but the wisdom of God never ordains anything without a purpose. Everything in this world is working for some great end. Fate does not say that...There is all the difference between fate and Providence that there is between a person with good eyes and a blind person.[12]

Unless they are atheists, most unbelievers fall into the first group. They are content to acknowledge that some higher power exists, but their pride and hard hearts will never allow them to concede that this higher power influences, much less controls, their lives and their futures. Sadly, even a few Christians fall into this group.

Most Christians fall into the second group. They're aware God has ultimate control over the larger events of the world and history. They believe in His prophecies but attribute them to His foreknowledge, believing He only *knows* the future rather than providentially *determines* the future. But their belief in His sovereignty becomes uncertain when they must decide where to draw the line regarding His control over smaller matters of everyday life, like our personal choices and the effects of sin and evil.

Few Christians are willing to venture into the third group. In fact, few have even heard the suggestion that no event — not the smallest, most meaningless moment of our everyday lives, every impulsive or well-considered personal decision, or even Satan's choices and actions — remains outside His direct and constant control. Yet ironically, when we all consider a great tragedy and ask, "How could a loving God allow such things?" we have unknowingly placed ourselves, if even for just a moment, into this group.

That very question assumes we believe that God *could* have changed the decisions and actions of two disturbed teenagers in Colorado. He could have altered the paths and opportunities of 19 terrorists and thousands of other people on September 11 to prevent destruction. He could have calmed the earthquake and held back the sea that devastated hundreds of thousands. Is it, in fact, true that God could have prevented these events?

The Bible says God is sovereign over the substance of the Creation: all weather, all the natural forces, all the animal kingdom. The Bible abounds with examples of His sovereignty. Nearly every book of the Old Testament credits God with producing bountiful harvests, famine, rain, drought, lightning and thunder, and life and death:

> *He sends forth His command to the earth; His Word runs very swiftly.*
>
> *He gives snow like wool; He scatters the frost like ashes.*
>
> *He casts forth His ice as fragments; who can stand before His cold?*
>
> *He sends forth His Word and melts them; He causes His wind to blow and the waters to flow.*
> —*Ps. 147:15-18*

The story of Moses in Egypt is a *tour de force* of God's sovereignty over the forces of nature, with hail, insects, animals, and even the heavens themselves responding in unison to God's command. In the Gospels, the Apostles watch as Jesus calms the storm on the sea of Galilee, and they declare that He commands even the wind and sea. In Daniel, God protects His servants from a fiery furnace and shuts lions' mouths. In Numbers, God speaks through the mouth of a donkey. In 1 Samuel, God causes two nursing cows yoked to a cart to deny their most urgent instincts and abandon their newborn young to return the Ark of the Covenant to Israel. There are many more examples, but we can easily conclude from these that there is no such thing as "mother nature." Nature has a Father, who will not share control.

> *For I know that the LORD is great and that our Lord is above all gods.*

> *Whatever the LORD pleases, He does, in Heaven and in earth, in the seas and in all deeps.*
> —*Ps. 135:5-6*

Now, you might be thinking that just because God can control all things doesn't mean He will exercise that control. Was God, for example, responsible for the tsunami discussed earlier? Did that tragedy occur because God made it happen, or did it happen by natural forces God merely allowed? This is a false dichotomy. Whether He actively causes or passively allows circumstances to occur is a distinction without a difference. Since Scripture tells us that even waves respond to God's Word (recall the flood of Noah), we also know He can stop these events if He wishes. He could have stopped that wave with one word from His mouth, just as He created all waters with His Word in the first place. Therefore, whether by initiating it or by not stopping it, in either case, He ordained it. It happened according to His will; otherwise, it would not have happened. It's like a child with a baseball that they tossed straight above their head, pondering as it fell whether to catch it or let it hit the ground. Whether they chose to act and reach out to catch the ball or chose to withhold action and allow the ball to hit the ground, either way, it was the child's choice and desire that determined the ball's fate. So it is with God.

The inescapable conclusion is that every natural event occurs because it is God's will. This stands true even in the greatest of calamities, because God tells us He deserves the credit:

> *I am the L*ORD*, and there is no other; besides Me there is no God. I will gird you, though you have not known Me; that people may know from the rising to the setting of the sun that there is no one besides Me. I am the L*ORD*, and there is no other, the One forming light and creating darkness, causing well-being and creating calamity; I am the L*ORD *who does all these.*
> —**Isa. 45:5-7**

> *If a trumpet is blown in a city will not the people tremble? If a calamity occurs in a city has not the LORD done it?*
> —**Amos 3:6**

Both Isaiah and Amos state the obvious: if we are prepared to give God credit for the good things that happen in His Creation, then we must be prepared to recognize that calamity also occurs on His watch, and by His will.

Part of our difficulty in accepting what God ordains stems from our concerns over the loss of innocent life. We find it hard to accept that God would allow, and even instigate, the loss of innocent lives. Our difficulty is not God or His nature, but our own wrong perspective. We may think of people as being good or innocent based on moral relativism, but that is a worldly and false understanding. God's definition of innocence and guilt, and what makes a death justified or unfair, is vastly different:

> *What then? Are we better than they? Not at all; for we have already charged that both Jews and Greeks are all under sin; as it is written, "*THERE IS NONE RIGHTEOUS, NOT EVEN ONE; THERE IS NONE WHO UNDERSTANDS, THERE IS NONE WHO SEEKS FOR

> GOD; ALL HAVE TURNED ASIDE, TOGETHER THEY HAVE BECOME USELESS; THERE IS NONE WHO DOES GOOD, THERE IS NOT EVEN ONE."
> —**Rom. 3:9-12**

> For whoever keeps the whole law and yet stumbles in one point, they have become guilty of all.
> —*James 2:10*

> For the wages of sin is death...
> —**Rom. 6:23**

The payment due to all who sin is death and does not depend on our conscious knowledge of our sinful state or our sinful deeds. Even the Law provides a sacrifice to cover unknown, unintentional sin. No, we all inherit our sin nature from Adam. God created Adam without sin, but once he sinned, he became a different creature: a fallen creature with a nature opposed to God. Since God had decreed during creation that every living creature would reproduce after its own kind, Adam's descendants would, by necessity, inherit his fallen nature. Every person ever born is born with Adam's dead nature, a corrupt and sinful nature opposed to God. Every person is guilty of sin even before they take their first breath, because our natural state is sinful. King David recognized this about himself when he wrote:

> Be gracious to me, O God, according to Your lovingkindness; according to the greatness of Your compassion blot out my transgressions.

> *Wash me thoroughly from my iniquity and cleanse me from my sin. For I know my transgressions, and my sin is ever before me. Against You, You only, I have sinned and done what is evil in Your sight, so that You are justified when You speak and blameless when You judge. Behold, I was brought forth in iniquity, and in sin my mother conceived me.*
> —*Ps. 51:1-5*

We can't understand how God could be responsible for, or even just allow, events that lead to death, in part because we fail to grasp the true depravity of the human heart — the degree to which the world justly deserves God's wrath. Prior to faith, there is never a moment in the life of any human being when he or she stands before God sinless and without blame. We were all conceived with a fallen nature, a nature opposed to God that, apart from faith, can never please Him. We all deserve judgment for that. In fact, there has only ever been one innocent life on earth: a man not born of Adam's seed and, therefore, without Adam's sinful nature, because He was born of the Holy Spirit through a virgin. Even that one innocent life ended in death by God's will after suffering great violence for the sake of the greater good. God has numbered our days, and He controls when, where, and how each life comes to an end — as is the Potter's right regarding His clay.

> *For we are His workmanship, created in Christ Jesus for good works, which God prepared beforehand so that we would walk in them.*
> —*Eph. 2:10*

This is a challenging topic. How could God prepare beforehand the decisions of people when our experience constantly tells us that we are the ones making our own decisions? How can He do that, knowing we make sinful decisions all the time? God is not the author of sin, but that doesn't mean He can't use it for His purposes. In truth, it's easy to find many examples of people in Scripture whose lives and decisions were directed and controlled by God. God used Pharaoh and his sin to display His glory throughout the world as He freed Israel from bondage (Exodus 8). He used Nebuchadnezzar and the Babylonian army to devastate Jerusalem and take the nation of Israel captive for 70 years as punishment for idol worship and ignoring land sabbaths (Daniel 1). God used the hatred of people in Jerusalem to scatter the early Church and spread the gospel message. None of them had a chance to object to how God decided to use them, nor did they even understand in the moment that God was in control and they were not.

One of the most famous examples of God's sovereignty over the events of men's lives is found in the story of Joseph. The story of Joseph begins in Genesis 15, when God confirms His covenant with Abram:

> *God said to Abram, "Know for certain that your descendants will be strangers in a land that is not theirs, where they will be enslaved and oppressed four hundred years. But I will also judge the nation whom they will serve, and afterward they will come out with many possessions."*

> "As for you, you shall go to your fathers in peace; you will be buried at a good old age. Then in the fourth generation they will return here, for the iniquity of the Amorite is not yet complete."
> —**Gen. 15:13-16**

Because the iniquity of the Amorites was not yet complete, God had Abram's descendants enslaved for four generations in a foreign land. God was not yet ready to judge the sin of the Canaanites who were living in the promised land, where their culture threatened the Jewish nation. This brings us to the story of Joseph.

God gives Joseph a dream, which Joseph then tells his elder brothers, saying that this dream revealed he would one day rule over them and their parents. Naturally, they become angry and jealous, plotting to destroy him so his dream can never come true. As the story develops in Genesis 37, Joseph's brothers seize an opportunity to sell Joseph to slave traders, which leads to a chain of events resulting in Joseph becoming Egypt's second in command. Meanwhile, the land of Canaan experiences a famine, which causes his brothers to go to Egypt in search of food. They come before Joseph, unaware of his identity. They (and later, their entire family) bow down before him, and the entire Jewish nation joins the brothers in Egypt and pays respect to Joseph. Thus, Joseph's dream is fulfilled.

The irony in this story is that the brothers believe their decision to sell Joseph into slavery will ensure his dream will never be realized, but instead, they ensure that it is. So, was it God or the brothers making these choices? Psalms provides the explanation:

> *He sent a man before them, Joseph, who was sold as a slave. They afflicted his feet with fetters, he himself was laid in irons; until the time that his Word came to pass, the Word of the LORD tested him. The king sent and released him, the ruler of peoples, and set him free. He made him lord of his house and ruler over all his possessions, to imprison his princes at will, that he might teach his elders wisdom.*
> ***—Ps. 105:17–22***

God, not the brothers, sent Joseph to Egypt. It was God's plan to test him through slavery and later imprisonment.

> *And God sent me before you to preserve a posterity for you in the earth, and to save your lives by a great deliverance. So now it was not you who sent me here, but God; and He has made me a father to Pharaoh, and lord of all his house, and a ruler throughout all the land of Egypt.*
> ***—Gen. 45:7–8***

> *But Joseph said to them, Do not be afraid, for am I in God's place? As for you, you meant evil against me, but God meant it for good in order to bring about this present result, to preserve many people alive.*
> ***—Gen. 50:19–20***

Fulfilling Joseph's dream was God's way of teaching Joseph's elders (his brothers) wisdom, but while their part in that fulfillment certainly had the desired effect, it does not mean God caused the brothers to sin. Rather, the brothers sinned because their hearts were depraved by nature. God then used the brother's sinful behavior to fulfill

His good purposes and reveal the consequences for their mistakes.

For many years afterward, the nation of Israel lived in Egypt. God wanted the Jewish people to continue to grow into a nation while remaining separate and uncorrupted by the world around them. Then, on the appointed day, Moses brought them out of Egypt: nearly 2 million of them, just as He had promised Abram 430 years earlier. When the time finally came for God to judge their enemy, the Amorites, He had an army of Israelites ready and willing to strike.

Consider the millions of people who made tens of millions of decisions in those 430 years ensuring this specific outcome would occur that specific day. Marriages were made, children were born, all the many details of life both great and small worked together so that everything happened as God intended. This is not simply God predicting the future; this is God obviously controlling the future in minute detail, to fulfill His word. And He's doing it today with the people on earth.

God has a preordained plan. Stories like these cause us to reconsider where we've drawn that line in the sand between God's control and ours. When we were unbelievers, we drew that line so far away we couldn't even see God, believing everything was under our control. Then, as we began to believe in Christ, that line came closer. Now, we must accept the truth and the power of God's Word, and move the line closer and closer until it's pressing up against us, pushing against our pride, staring us in the face and asking, "Who are you, that you would dare to draw any line between you and God?" We would be wise to acknowledge in truth that God is sovereign over the stick, the sand, and us.

> *O Lord, You have searched me and known me.*
>
> *You know when I sit down and when I rise up;*
>
> *You understand my thought from afar.*
>
> *You scrutinize my path and my lying down,*
>
> *And are intimately acquainted with all my ways.*
>
> *Even before there is a word on my tongue,*
>
> *Behold, O Lord, You know it all.*
>
> *You have enclosed me behind and before,*
>
> *And laid Your hand upon me.*
>
> *Such knowledge is too wonderful for me;*
>
> *It is too high, I cannot attain to it.*
>
> —**Ps. 139:1–6**

CHAPTER SEVEN

Experience Over Scripture

Throughout this book, we've examined various aspects of God's sovereignty over His Creation, specifically regarding prayer, wealth and health, evangelism, and world events. We've confronted the church's immaturity in understanding and promoting issues including:

- the belief that the purpose of prayer is to give God new thoughts, vs. the *biblical* teaching that the purpose of prayer is to give *us* new thoughts;
- the belief that God's desire is to give us material wealth in this lifetime, vs. the *biblical* teaching that God's desire is for us to spend freely our worldly wealth to build treasure in heaven;
- the belief that physical health is a way to measure God's approval, vs. the *biblical* teaching that those most committed to living their faith

obediently usually face the greatest earthly trials and sufferings;

- twisting the Great Commission into a marketing initiative designed to create new believers, vs. the *biblical* teaching that only God can create faith, while the Church is called only to baptize and make disciples of new believers;
- lacking appreciation for God's control over all things, and as a result, fearing world events, vs. the *biblical* teaching of resting on scriptural promises that tell us never to fear, but to trust God's goodness and His promise to work all things to the good for those who love Him and are called according to His purpose.

We examined the truth of Scripture for the correct biblical perspective on each topic. Truth is found in His word, and that truth is completely and entirely sufficient for all our needs, concerns, and instruction. Now we turn to an important topic in the exploration of God's sovereignty: the power of God's Word to do the greatest work of all — transform our hearts.

Walk into a bookstore today and you will find that one of the fastest-growing non-fiction genres is self-help, or books promising solutions to all of life's problems. These books are often secular, using principles drawn from modern psychology, new age mysticism, medicine, and other sources. Gurus like Oprah and Dr. Phil attempt to solve urgent life problems by rearranging our thinking and our organizational skills, or by building our self-esteem and helping us leave things behind — whatever might get us in a right frame of mind. A notable subset of this genre is Christian-focused self-help. These books promise to help Christians live the good life, walk in Christ's footsteps, live their faith obediently, and get closer to God. The world is hooked on self-help bestsellers, believers included. Why are these self-help books so popular among Christians?

The Church has truly come to resemble the world. Judging by how many social problems and persistent sins we share with the unsaved world, it's fair to say that the Church is sick, weak, and stunted in maturity. As a result, it is often ineffective in its commission and calling. If you think that's an overstatement, consider these statistics:

- The Christian divorce rate is higher than in the unbelieving world.[13]

- Individual Christians and Christian churches declare bankruptcy at the same rate as the unchurched.[14]

- Among never-married fundamentalist adults between 2008 and 2018, 86% of females and 82% of males had at least one opposite-sex sexual partner since age 18, while 57% and 65%, respectively, had three or more.[15]

- In 2017, the CDC reported 30% of high school students drank some amount of alcohol within the last 30 days, 14% binge drank, 6% drove after drinking, and 17% rode with a driver who had drunk alcohol.[16]

- Thirty percent of Christians report physical or sexual abuse by spouses.[17]

Many believe the true numbers are even higher since Christians feel guilty about their behavior and are therefore less likely to self-report. Nevertheless, it should not be surprising that Christians experience life's failures at virtually the same rate as unbelievers when we so often seek help from the same sources. Christians today commonly read the same books as their unbelieving neighbors, watch the same television programs, follow the same fads, and invest time studying the same powerless teachings. As a result, we end up just as spiritually malnourished as the unbelieving world. Because we've largely set aside what makes us different, so many in the Church have difficulty living a life that's set apart — a life that shows the world the victory we've already won in Christ. We've set aside the very source of that power: he Word, Christ Himself. We've set aside the sufficiency of the Word of God.

In the first-century Church, the writer to the Hebrews was contending with a similar problem. Before explaining a complicated issue concerning Melchizedek, the high priest from Genesis 14, the writer pauses to admonish the particular church he is addressing:

> *Concerning him we have much to say, and it is hard to explain, since you have become dull of hearing. For though by this time you ought to be teachers, you have need again for someone to teach you the elementary principles of the oracles of God, and you have come to need milk and not*

> *solid food. For everyone who partakes only of milk is not accustomed to the word of righteousness, for they are infants. But solid food is for the mature, who because of practice have their senses trained to discern good and evil.*
> —**Heb. 5:11-14**

> *Therefore leaving the elementary teaching about the Christ, let us press on to maturity, not laying again a foundation of repentance from dead works and of faith toward God, of instruction about washings and laying on of hands, and the resurrection of the dead and eternal judgment. And this we will do, if God permits.*
> —**Heb. 6:1-3**

The writer pauses in his discussion of Melchizedek because he is frustrated at how immature and unprepared this church is for that topic. In fact, this church's immaturity extends beyond a poor understanding of Melchizedek. He writes that they have become dull of hearing. The Greek word he uses is *nothros*, meaning "sluggish" or "lazy." This church is not accustomed to the hard work of hearing and studying Gods' truth, so they can't appreciate advanced teachings. This isn't a matter of ability, training, spiritual gifting, or role in the Church. This is a matter of effort, diligence, and commitment to maturing. Had they been diligent to study, they would be able to teach others difficult subjects, but they are far from able, and he scolds them for it. He isn't suggesting they all should have the spiritual gift of teaching, or even a teaching role. He is merely pointing out they should have applied themselves to obtaining enough knowledge and understanding that, if called upon, they could teach someone else.

This church is so spiritually immature that they need remedial education. They have forgotten the little they learned and need to again be taught elementary principles from the Word of God. Like infants, they need to return to milk rather than moving on to solid food. An infant who is fed solid food before it is ready will die. It will choke, or its digestive tract will not be able to process the food and it will starve. Infants must have something easy to digest — something simple yet nourishing. Milk is the perfect food for an infant, but at some point, milk alone becomes insufficient. The child can't continue to grow without more complex foods. The food that sustained it in its early years can't continue to fuel its growth to maturity. Thus, if that child continues to be fed only milk and not solid food, its body will grow anemic. The once perfect nourishment becomes insufficient for the body's growth and maturity, and when taken long enough without additional, solid food, it will cause death. Growth will cease, strength will fade, sight will grow dim, and life will be extinguished. This is the writer's concern for the Hebrew church. They received the essential teachings of the Church — they received their milk — but when it came time to mature, they never progressed to solid food. They remain stunted, feeding on the elementary teachings. In fact, they've left even those aside, which is why the writer says they need to relearn those lessons. By perpetually existing on milk, they have stunted their growth, and their very existence as a church is in question.

In Hebrews 6:1–2, the writer defines the milk of elementary principles that all Christians need from their earliest days of faith:

First, we need to teach the need to repent from dead works and show faith toward God — this is the gospel message. It is important to teach new Christians how the Holy Spirit changed them and what it means to have grace by faith. They should understand that good works are the response to salvation, rather than the means by which they are saved.

Second, we should teach about baptisms, anointings, and giftings; the works of the Holy Spirit. The writer says these teachings are milk, things that even the newest Christian should learn and understand. Once Christians understands the gospel message, they should move on to maturity, but many Christians remain utterly confused about what the Bible says regarding the spiritual giftings, the purpose and meaning of baptism, and the role of the Holy Spirit in the life of the Body of Christ.

Third, we should teach the resurrection of the dead with an understanding that our destiny is to be resurrected in bodily form to reign with Christ on earth for a thousand years. This should be an elementary teaching for all Christians.

Finally, we must teach eternal judgment. Scripture teaches that all unbelievers will also be resurrected into a new body so they may be judged and suffer the penalty for their sin in the Lake of Fire.

These are the elementary teachings that every Christian should learn in Christianity 101, but few Christians can understand, much less teach, these biblical principles. In fact, there are pastors who can't adequately explain these doctrines. Christians often attend their regular weekly service hoping to be edified by the meat of the Word only to discover that the message is just another exhortation to repent and believe in the gospel. Or worse, there is no teaching of the Word of God at all. There is no challenge to press on to maturity. Thus, it is fair to compare the Church today to the Hebrew church that received this letter. Spiritual infants fill the pews of most churches today, slowly dying on milk, when they need the meat of the Word of God. Somewhere along the way, churches came up with the crazy idea that only pastors need to understand the Word in depth, but pastors should share their knowledge with their congregations. The only medicine that can heal the sickness of sin is disciplined, in-depth study of the Word of God:

> *But solid food is for the mature, who because of practice have their senses trained to discern good and evil.*
> **—Heb. 5:14**

As this verse states, those who don't mature beyond the milk of the Word cannot discern good from evil. An undiscerning church won't recognize bad teaching and will likely fall prey to those encouraging a return to the Law, as was the case with the Hebrew church. Such a church may succumb to false teaching on prosperity, healing, prayer, and other difficult issues. A church that cannot discern the good teaching of Scripture from the evil teaching of the unbelieving world will embrace its views on issues like evolution, the Word of Faith movement, and new age spirituality in all its forms. The enemy of the Word comes as an angel of light and is spiritually discerned. If the

Church cannot discern good from evil, then we have no hope of demonstrating that our lives are different because of Christ, the Spirit, and the Word. God's sovereignty over His church and its members begins and ends with the sufficiency of the Word of God.

We know from Romans 10 that faith comes when the Holy Spirit applies the Word of Christ to an unbeliever's heart. And Scripture teaches that God uses the Word to mold us and conform us to the likeness of Christ.

> *But Christ, after He had offered one sacrifice for sins forever, sat down at the right hand of God, from that time waiting till His enemies are made His footstool. For by one offering He has perfected forever those who are being sanctified.*
> **—Heb. 10:12-14**

By offering Himself on the cross, Christ *perfected* believers forever — past tense. It is finished. Our perfection before the Father is complete. We stand blameless before Him, not by our own account, but by Christ's account. His perfection is applied to us. It's a contradiction to think we can take something perfect and make it more perfect. The scripture is speaking of our *position* before God, versus our *nature*. Though we are perfect in our position before the Father, we must still be sanctified — made holy and set apart — because we still experience imperfection and sin in our lives. God wants to remove sin from us every bit as much as He has already removed its penalty. He's not satisfied for us to stand sinless before Him in Christ: He still expects us to seek perfection in our lives, even while we wait to be glorified. The Word of God accomplishes both our justification and our sanctification.

> *Husbands, love your wives, just as Christ also loved the Church and gave Himself up for her, so that He might sanctify her, having cleansed her by the washing of water with the Word...*
> —**Eph. 5:25-26**

Christ's death on the cross was the means to an end. If we stop at justification, we frustrate the work of God in us. Peter encouraged the early Church in much the same way:

> *...like newborn babies, long for the pure milk of the Word, so that by it you may grow in respect to salvation...*
> —**1 Pet. 2:2**

The Word of God will make believers grow after salvation by enabling them to demonstrate the perfection they obtained through Christ. There's an often-told story of how God provides for our needs even when we don't recognize His provision:

A farmer's house is flooded, and he crawls onto the roof of his barn to escape the flood waters. Multiple rescue crafts float by offering aid, but he turns them down, stating that God will save him. A helicopter even tries to save him, but he refuses, insisting that God will save him. Ultimately, he dies in the flood. When he arrives in Heaven, he asks God why He didn't send help. God responds by saying, "I sent three boats and a helicopter, what more did you want?"

Many in the Church today are sitting on top of that farmhouse. Our congregations suffer crumbling marriages, but they get their advice from Oprah and then wonder why the Church's divorce rate is no different from world's. Our congregations feel the stress and emptiness of hectic and over-committed lives, but they turn to Dr. Phil for answers and wonder why church participation plummets. Our people come to church looking for direction and purpose, but we give them a six-week program and a bestselling hardback, and six months later we wonder why nothing seems to have changed. Our children stray into worldly behaviors and thinking, and we respond with youth programs that are little more than MTV concerts or summer parties. Then we wonder why so few bear spiritual fruit and so many leave the Church altogether by the time they're adults. As the flood reaches our rooftops, and one congregation after another succumbs, we watch and wonder why God doesn't do something to preserve His church.

This story of the rich man and Lazarus reflects this disregard for God's Word. The rich man (an unbeliever) is in torment while Lazarus (a faithful man) is attended by Abraham in comfort. The rich man recognizes that his family is in danger of his same fate if they don't believe, so he asks Abraham to send Lazarus to warn his family:

> *And he said, "Then I beg you, father, that you send him to my father's house — for I have five brothers — in order that he may warn them, so that they will not also come to*

> *this place of torment."*
>
> *But Abraham said, "They have Moses and the Prophets; let them hear them."*
>
> *But he said, "No, father Abraham, but if someone goes to them from the dead, they will repent!"*
>
> *But he said to him, "If they do not listen to Moses and the Prophets, they will not be persuaded even if someone rises from the dead."*
>
> —**Luke 16:27-31**

Abraham tells the rich man that his brothers can look to Moses and the Prophets — the Scriptures — for their warning. But the rich man says that's not enough, because his brothers have dismissed that wisdom and need something more spectacular to convince them hell is real. Abraham assures him that if the Word of God isn't enough, nothing else will work. If the Word of God isn't enough to address our hardships, weaknesses, and failures, nothing else will work for us, either. As we sit atop our farmhouse waiting for another self-help guru to save us, or more *Chicken Soup for the Soul*, or another book *about* the Bible, one by one we will drown waiting for a solution that never comes.

As Hebrews teaches, without a commitment to study and spend time in the Word, we have no hope of understanding the truth, much less choosing good over evil and overcoming the consequences of a life marked by wrong choices. God's sovereign choice is to use His word and nothing else to accomplish His work in this world. It is His word that goes out, and it will not return void. It is His word through which He created all things and by which

He sustains all things. It is by His word that He will make His church holy, as it is written in the Psalms:

> *I will worship toward Your holy temple, and praise Your name for Your lovingkindness and Your truth; for You have magnified Your Word above all Your name.*
> —*Ps. 138:2*

God has magnified His word even above His name. He won't give satisfaction to those who forsake His word and seek answers elsewhere. The sovereignty of God means He chooses to work miracles in the lives of His people through His word, rather than by other means, so that when the work is done, He will rightly receive the glory. As we cry to God asking why He has left us to despair in our sinful and hurting lives, the Father stands before us saying, "I sent you the best help I could: I sent you my Son, the Word. He is in you now in the form of my Spirit, and He is before you now on the pages of that Book. Every page testifies to His power and sufficiency." And yet, we so often set our Bible aside. It sits on our shelf like a reference book or a dictionary we occasionally open to look up a passage.

The Body of Christ is weak and anemic because somewhere along the way, we individually pushed the Word of God aside and made its study and understanding the responsibility of our pastors — a role many have abdicated. We've declared the Bible useless and out of step with our times. We would rather turn to the newsstand and our horoscopes for relationship advice. We don't have the patience to let God's Word guide us through our struggles over our lifetime. We would rather read the latest paperback book about the Bible than invest the time and effort to read and study the Bible itself. One pastor even declared from the pulpit that one of his chief concerns was that his congregation was spending too much time in Bible studies. He preferred they spend more time in home groups where they rarely opened a Bible, and where the leaders knew little or nothing of Scripture but were expected to counsel the group on all of life's challenges — the blind leading the blind.

Of course, we shouldn't abandon all other church activities, but Bible study should be our priority over other pursuits. Spending time in God's Word should be on par with all the other seemingly important things in a Christian's schedule. This isn't an either/or proposition, but rather a matter of using the proper tool for the job. If our job is repairing broken lives, building up the faithful, equipping the saints for ministry, and training in righteousness, then our tool is the Word of God:

> *All Scripture is inspired by God and profitable for teaching, for reproof, for correction, for training in righteousness; so that the person of God may be adequate, equipped for every good work.*
> **—2 Tim. 3:16-17**

We must rely on the sovereignty of God and the sufficiency of His Word if we truly want to see revival and see God's people changed. To achieve that goal, we must demand our leadership inspire us in that way, revering the sovereignty of God and seeking guidance for our lives in His word, as did King Josiah:

> *Josiah was eight years old when he became king, and he reigned thirty-one years in Jerusalem; and his mother's name was Jedidah the daughter of Adaiah of Bozkath.*
>
> *He did right in the sight of the LORD and walked in all the way of his father David, nor did he turn aside to the right or to the left. Now in the eighteenth year of King Josiah, the king sent Shaphan, the son of Azaliah the son of Meshullam the scribe, to the house of the LORD saying, Go up to Hilkiah the high priest that he may count the money brought in to the house of the LORD which the doorkeepers have gathered from the people. Let them deliver it into the hand of the workmen who have the oversight of the house of the LORD, and let them give it to the workmen who are in the house of the LORD to repair the damages of the house, to the carpenters and the builders and the masons and for buying timber and hewn stone to repair the house. Only no accounting shall be made with them for the money delivered into their hands, for they deal faithfully.*
> —*2 Kings 22:1-6*

The nation of Israel experienced years of pain under poor leadership. Past kings had led Israel to worship idols, which then led to widespread apostasy. The Word of God had all but disappeared from among His chosen people. The temple was in disrepair, the sacrifices had ceased, and idols were everywhere. Since the people had forgotten the Word of God and had not hidden it in their hearts, they no longer knew the difference between good and evil and therefore followed their flesh. But God raised up Josiah, who lived like David, turning neither to his right nor to his left. Desiring to restore God's temple, Josiah instructed the priest to make the repairs using the money given in idol worship. Further, the priest should not ask the workmen to account for the money they received, because anyone Josiah trusted to repair God's temple could certainly be trusted to manage the money for the assignment. So, the repair work began:

> Then Hilkiah the high priest said to Shaphan the scribe, "I have found the book of the law in the house of the LORD." And Hilkiah gave the book to Shaphan who read it.
>
> Shaphan the scribe came to the king and brought back word to the king and said, "Your servants have emptied out the money that was found in the house, and have delivered it into the hand of the workmen who have the oversight of the house of the LORD." Moreover, Shaphan the scribe told the king saying, "Hilkiah the priest has given me a book." And Shaphan read it in the presence of the king.
>
> When the king heard the words of the book of the law, he tore his clothes.
>
> Then the king commanded Hilkiah the priest, Ahikam the son of Shaphan, Achbor the son of Micaiah, Shaphan the scribe, and Asaiah the king's servant saying, "Go, inquire of the LORD for me and the people and all Judah concerning the words of this book that has been found, for great is the wrath of the LORD that burns against us, because our fathers have not listened to the words of this book, to do according to all that is written concerning us."
> —*2 Kings 22:8-13*

During the work, the workmen made a curious discovery: the scroll of the Word of God — specifically, the Law of Moses. The king immediately appreciated the importance of this find, and he tore his clothes in mourning and distress. However, the words of the Law were so foreign to his ears that he asked the priest to inquire what they meant and if he could discern God's verdict on Israel's disobedience. What would God say to His people about how they had treated His word, about how they had tossed it aside and buried it beneath their idol worship? The answer came through a prophetess, Huldah: God would bring judgment for those who had trampled His word, but He would bring relief in Josiah's day because the king had a heart for God's Word and respect for His power. Josiah humbled his heart and wept before God, because he felt the same pain our Father feels at the thought of His people rejecting His word.

If we seek the power to live our faith obediently, to know the peace that surpasses all understanding, and to hear the Lord say on the day of our glorification, "Well done, good and faithful servant," then we need only to spend time with Him, in His care and under His instruction, through His Word. Service is good, fellowship is helpful, prayer is important, home groups have their place, and the Christian bestseller list may offer encouragement from time to time, but the sovereignty of God means that *only* His word has the power to change who you are, what you do, and how you think.

As you seek guidance for your Christian walk, consider this: if a teacher has no delight in exploring the mysteries hidden in the Word of God, and presents only a diet of milk without an exhortation to study, then no matter how entertaining or motivational that teacher's sermon, it will lack the power to bring maturity and growth, for they come in their own power, not God's. Seek instead teachers who devote themselves to Scripture, who believe that God's Word is the solution for that which troubles the soul, and who weep with Josiah when the people discard God's Word — for such teachers come with God's power. God is sovereign over all His Creation, including you. As you seek His will and purpose for your life, turn to the Word and rely on His guidance through the Holy Spirit. Take comfort in knowing that He wants to be known and that He will never leave or forsake us. Use the discernment He gives through the study of His word to seek teachers who respect the sufficiency of God's Word, so that through such teaching, you may grow in the grace and knowledge of our Lord Jesus Christ.

> *How blessed is the one who does not walk in the counsel of the wicked, nor stand in the path of sinners, nor sit in the seat of scoffers! But their delight is in the law of the LORD, and in His law they meditate day and night. They will be like a tree firmly planted by streams of water, which yields its fruit in its season and its leaf does not wither; and in whatever they do, they prosper. The wicked are not so, but they are like chaff which the wind drives away. Therefore, the wicked will not stand in the judgment, nor sinners in the assembly of the righteous. For the LORD knows the way of the righteous, but the way of the wicked will perish.*
> **—Ps. 1:1-6**

Works Cited

1. Olsteen, J. *Your Best Life Now: 7 Steps to Living at Your Full Potential.* FaithWords, 2014.

2. Olsteen, J. (2014). *Your Best Life Now: 7 Steps to Living at Your Full Potential.* New York: FaithWords

3. Barna Group. (2018, July 10). *State of the Bible 2018: Seven Top Findings.* Retrieved from https://www.barna.com/research/state-of-the-bible-2018-seven-top-findings/

4. Barna Group. (2018, July 10). *State of the Bible 2018: Seven Top Findings.* Retrieved from https://www.barna.com/research/state-of-the-bible-2018-seven-top-findings/

5. Barna Group. (2009, December 20). *Barna Studies the Research, Offers a Year-in-Review Perspective.* Retrieved from https://www.barna.com/research/barna-studies-the-research-offers-a-year-in-review-perspective/

6. Barna Group. (2009, December 20). *Barna Studies the Research, Offers a Year-in-Review Perspective.* Retrieved from https://www.barna.com/research/barna-studies-the-research-offers-a-year-in-review-perspective/

7. Barna Group. (2009, December 20). *Barna Studies the Research, Offers a Year-in-Review Perspective*. Retrieved from https://www.barna.com/research/barna-studies-the-research-offers-a-year-in-review-perspective/

8. Barna Group. (2009, December 20). *Barna Studies the Research, Offers a Year-in-Review Perspective*. Retrieved from https://www.barna.com/research/barna-studies-the-research-offers-a-year-in-review-perspective/

9. Barna Group. (2009, December 20). *Barna Studies the Research, Offers a Year-in-Review Perspective*. Retrieved from https://www.barna.com/research/barna-studies-the-research-offers-a-year-in-review-perspective/

10. The Barna Group. (2005, August 9). Most Adults Feel Accepted by God, But Lack a Biblical Worldview. Ventura, CA, USA.

11. Spurgeon, C. H. (1857). *Sermons of the Rev. C. H. Spurgeon of London.* New York: Sheldon, Blakeman & Company.

12. Spurgeon, C. H. (1857). *Sermons of the Rev. C. H. Spurgeon of London.* New York: Sheldon, Blakeman & Company.

13. Stepler, R. (2017, March 9). Led by Baby Boomers, divorce rates climb for America's 50+ population. Washington, DC, USA: Pew Research Center.

14. (Foohey, et al., June 2017) (Foohey, 2018)

15. Ayers, D. J. (2019, August 14). Sex and the Single Evangelical. Grove City, Pennsylvania, USA.

16. Division of Population Health , National Center for Chronic Disease Prevention and Health Promotion , Centers for Disease Control and Prevention, 2018

17. Westenberg, L. (2017, July 7). *'When She Calls for Help'— Domestic Violence in Christian Families.* Retrieved from MDPI: Social Sciences: https://www.mdpi.com/2076-0760/6/3/71/htm

About the Author

Stephen Armstrong was the founder and principal teacher of Verse By Verse Ministry International. He came to know the Lord in his early 30s, while serving as an Air Force officer. After becoming a believer, Stephen experienced God's call to learn and teach the Bible, so in 1997 Stephen left the military, found a job in Colorado, and began a self-directed course of study in preparation to teach the scriptures.

As he devoted himself to study, Stephen developed a love for an in-depth, verse-by-verse style of teaching God's Word, believing it to be the best means to persuade the unbeliever of the truth of the Gospel and equip the saints for the work of ministry (Rom 10:17; Eph 4:14-15).

In 2001, Stephen received God's call to move to San Antonio, Texas, where he soon found opportunities to teach and preach verse-by-verse in churches throughout the area. Despite having no professional religious training, in 2003 Stephen was called by God to lead a church planting effort in the city as pastor of Living Word Fellowship.

That same year he also founded Verse By Verse Ministry of San Antonio (later to be renamed Verse By Verse Ministry International) out of a desire to offer his unique style of in-depth Bible teaching for free to a worldwide audience via the internet. Today, VBVMI's worldwide reach and growing catalog of insightful Bible teaching is proof that the Lord calls unqualified people but does not leave them untrained.

Stephen passed away in January 2021 leaving behind a library of insightful Bible teaching and a ministry team committed to advancing the Gospel worldwide.

Stephen is survived by his wife Annette and two adult children.

Made in the USA
Coppell, TX
06 October 2021